Catalogue of Sikh Coins in the British Museum

Paramdip Kaur Khera

**British Museum Research Publication
Number 190**

Publishers
The British Museum
Great Russell Street
London WC1B 3DG

Managing Editor: Dr Josephine Turquet
Assistant Editor: Sarah Wray

Distributors
The British Museum Press
46 Bloomsbury Street
London WC1B 3QQ

Catalogue of Sikh Coins in the British Museum
Paramdip Kaur Khera

ISBN 978 086159 190 9
ISSN 1747 3640

© The Trustees of the British Museum 2011

Front cover: Gold double mohur, British Museum 1912,0709.210
Bleazby collection. See catalogue no. 2, p. 22.

Note: the British Museum Occasional Papers series is now entitled
British Museum Research Publications. The OP series runs from
1 to 150, and the RP series, keeping the same ISSN and ISBN
preliminary numbers, begins at number 151.

For a complete catalogue of the full range of OPs and RPs see the series
website: www.britishmuseum.org/research/research_publications.aspx

Order from www.britishmuseum.org/shop
For trade orders write to:
Oxbow Books,
10 Hythe Bridge Street, Oxford, OX1 2EW,
UK
Tel: (+44) (0) 1865 241249
e-mail oxbow@oxbowbooks.com
website www.oxbowbooks.com
or
The David Brown Book Co
PO Box 511, Oakville
CT 06779, USA
Tel: (+1) 860 945 9329; Toll free 1 800 791 9354
e mail david.brown.bk.co@snet.net

Printed and bound in the UK by 4edge Ltd, Hockley

Contents

Acknowledgements	iv
Introduction	1
Chapter 1. Historical Context	2
Chapter 2. Sikh Mints	9
Chapter 3. Denominations and Circulation	14
Chapter 4. Coin Inscriptions	16
Chapter 5. Dates and Symbols on Sikh Coins	19
Chapter 6. Catalogue	22
Appendices	73
Appendix 1: Sikh, Mughal and Afghan rulers	73
Appendix 2: Mint Marks on Sikh Coins	75
Appendix 3: Gurmukhi and Persian Numerals	77
Appendix 4: Vikrama Samvat Conversion Chart	77
Glossary	78
Bibliography	80
Index	81

Dedicated to the *Khalsa Panth*

Acknowledgements

There are several individuals I would like to acknowledge who have supported me during the process of writing this catalogue. First and foremost I would like to thank Joe Cribb (former Keeper of Coins and Medals) for encouraging me to publish the collection of Sikh coins and for his constant support throughout my tenure at the British Museum.

I am especially grateful to my colleagues Helen Wang, Vesta Curtis and Elizabeth Errington; this catalogue could not have been written without their enthusiasm, continuous encouragement and friendship. Credit is due to Sushma Jansari for her guidance, assistance and suggestions for this publication and to Palwinder Mander for her cooperation and constructive feedback.

I would also like to thank Laura Phillips and Kirstin Leighton-Boyce for helping me to promote and highlight the Sikh collections within the Museum.

Harbinder Singh, Director of the Anglo-Sikh Heritage Trail first introduced me to the Sikh coin collection at the British Museum in 2005, an event which was pivotal in my research and has resulted in this long-awaited catalogue.

Josephine Turqet has helped me to transform my initial ideas into this publication for which I am most thankful.

I would like to acknowledge my husband, Harwinder Singh for his support and patience with tedious questions and to the rest of my family and friends who have been waiting for this work.

Finally, I would like to thank my Father, Ravinder Singh Khera who encouraged me to read Sikh history from a young age and inspired me to be proud of my heritage.

Paramdip Kaur Khera
The British Museum
December 2011

Portrait of Maharaja Ranjit Singh seated on a terrace (ruled 1801–39 AD). Painted in gouache on paper, c. 1830. British Museum, 1920,0917,0.227

Introduction

The study of Sikh coins has seen a recent resurgence in interest and popularity after being somewhat neglected and overlooked in the past. It is increasingly recognised that Sikh coinage is a valuable tool that can help to understand more fully the social and political changes that took place in the Punjab during the 18th and 19th centuries. Furthermore, these coins provide a unique insight into the short-lived, yet influential and historically significant, Sikh kingdom.

Currently, there are a limited number of publications that focus on Sikh coinage. The more recent works include Hans Herrli's *Coins of the Sikhs* (New Delhi, 2004) and Surinder's Singh's *Sikh Coinage – A Symbol of Sikh Sovereignty* (New Delhi, 2004). Herrli's detailed catalogue was the first, and remains the only, comprehensive catalogue of its kind. This underlines the importance of Herrli's work for the study of Sikh numismatics. Publications such as these, coupled with new research, have rendered much of the earlier literature relating to Sikh coins somewhat out of date.

It is hoped that the publication of the British Museum's Sikh coins, one of the world's greatest collections, will introduce this material to a wider audience. It will also provide academic and amateur numismatists alike with a detailed reference work which can be used to identify Sikh coins more precisely.

The British Museum's Sikh coin collection comprises over 500 coins which have been attributed to the Sikh Misal period (1760–1801) and the kingdom of Maharaja Ranjit Singh (1801–49). Silver rupees and copper coins make up the majority of the collection and most of these were minted in the Sikh holy city of Amritsar. Lahore, Kashmir, Multan and Peshawar are among the other important mints represented.

In terms of provenance, the coins came from a variety of sources and collections. Several Sikh coins were collected by British officials and army personnel who served in India in the late 19th and 20th centuries and later donated or sold their coins to the British Museum. These individuals include George B. Bleazby, Charles J. Rodgers and Richard B. Whitehead.

Approximately 250 coins are from the Bleazby collection. George Bernard Bleazby worked for the Financial Department of the Government of India and was made Assistant Accountant General of the Punjab in January 1902.[1] He was a keen coin collector with a particular expertise in North Indian coins and donated much of his collection to the Sri Partap Museum in Srinagar, Kashmir and also to the Lahore Museum. In commemoration of the Delhi Durbar in 1911, Henry Van Den Bergh, a member of the Executive Committee of the National Art Collections Fund, presented over 25,000 of Bleazby's coins, including the Sikh coins to the British Museum.

Charles James Rodgers (1838–98) sold a number of Sikh coins that he owned to the British Museum in 1897. He had set up a teacher training college in Amritsar in 1863 and was Principal there for 22 years. He studied Indian and Persian numismatics and wrote one of the very first articles to be published on Sikh coins in 1881.[2]

Richard Bertram Whitehead (1879–1967) was a member of the Indian Civil Service and wrote a number of books on Indian numismatics, including the *Catalogue of Coins in the Punjab Museum, Lahore* (1914). The British Museum purchased the Whitehead collection in 1922.

After the 1858 Government of India Act, East India Company rule in India ended and the British Raj assumed responsibility for Indian rule and administration. As part of this change, the India Museum in London was also brought under the India Office's jurisdiction. This museum closed in 1879 and its considerable collections, which included Sikh coins, were transferred to the British Museum between 1880 and 1882.

This new catalogue focuses on coins that circulated as currency and includes coins from various Sikh mints that were issued by the Sikh Misals and Ranjit Singh. For this reason, it does not include coins from the cis-Sutlej[3] states issued by the Maharajas of Patiala and Nabha, nor those of the Dogra Rajas in Jammu and Kashmir. Medals, tokens and commemorative coins are also not included.

In addition to an overview of Sikh history, from the founding of the religion in 1469 to the annexation of the Punjab by the British in 1849, the development of the Sikh faith will be outlined through short biographies of the Sikh Gurus. This is important because the Sikh Misals and Ranjit Singh were influenced by the Sikh religious philosophy and way of life and this, in turn, had an impact on the coinage that they issued. An introduction to the coins will provide information about their denominations, mints, inscriptions, dates and symbols. This will be followed by the catalogue of the collection.

Notes
1. *The Gazette of India*. 8 February 1902, 109–10. Leave and Appointments, Calcutta. 6 February 1902: 'Mr G.B. Bleazby – Chief Superintendent of the office of the Accountant General Punjab is promoted to class V of the enrolled list, with effect from the 1st January 1902, and is posted as Assistant Accountant General, Punjab'.
2. Rodgers, 1881, 71–93.
3. Cis-Sutlej refers to the region south of the river Sutlej.

Chapter 1
Historical Context

The Sikh Gurus

Guru Nanak 1469–1539

Guru Nanak founded the Sikh faith. He was born in 1469 to a small Khatri family, in the village of Talwandi close to Lahore in modern-day Pakistan.[1] His father, Mehta Kalu, is believed to have been responsible for assessing the crop revenue of Rai Bular Bhatti's land in the region.[2]

Nanaki, Guru Nanak's sister, spent a great deal of time with her brother throughout his life and provided him with her constant support. At the age of 16, Guru Nanak moved to Sultanpur to live with his newly married sister and found work with the Governor of Lahore, Daulat Khan Lodhi. Guru Nanak was entrusted with the task of weighing grain[3] and keeping records of the weight in the *Modikhana*.[4]

According to the *Janam Sakhis*, accounts of Guru Nanak's life which are thought to have been written by his companion Bhai Bala, Guru Nanak was spiritually aware from a very young age. As a young adult he spent much of his time talking with saints and holy men and made an effort to feed the poor in a free kitchen, or *langar*. One such example is known as the *Sacha Sauda*, 'true transaction'. Mehta Kalu gave his son 20 rupees advising him to make a good investment or business transaction with the money. On his way to a village outside of Talwandi, Guru Nanak met a group of *Sadhus*, 'mendicants' who were hungry. Nanak felt that there was no better way of spending the money than to feed the hungry holy men. He spent all of the money that his father had given to him on food for the mendicants and then returned home.[5]

Guru Nanak was born at a time when many people in northern India suffered religious and social persecution under the Mughal Emperor Babur. In response to this, Guru Nanak preached a message of truth, equality and justice. His teachings were strictly monotheistic and focused on universal humanism and freedom of expression. In contrast to existing practices, Guru Nanak preached both the equality of women with men and the removing of class and caste barriers which were then prevalent in society.

Guru Nanak's ideology can be summarised as follows:

Sat, Santokh, vichaar: truth, contentment and reflection;
Daya, dharma, dan: compassion, righteousness and charity;
Sidak, sabar, sanjam: faith, tolerance and restraint;
Khima, garibi, seva: forgiveness, humility and service;
Gyan, kirt: knowledge and work.

This ideology influenced Guru Nanak's devotees and formed the foundation of Sikhism.

Throughout his life, Guru Nanak emphasised the equality of Hindus and Muslims. To this end, he often sang hymns in praise of God alongside his close companions, Bhai Mardana (a Muslim) and Bhai Bala (a Hindu). He travelled all over India from the north, including the Punjab, the Gangetic plains and the Himalayas, to the south, from the Deccan to Sri Lanka, as well as through, the north-west as far as Afghanistan and Iraq.

Towards the end of his life, Guru Nanak appointed as his successor Bhai Lehna, a committed devotee, who became the second Sikh Guru, Guru Angad.

Guru Angad, 1539–52

Guru Angad continued to preach Guru Nanak's message and established over 100 *sangats*, 'congregations'. In keeping with the founding Guru's philosophy, Guru Angad rejected the Brahmanical Hindu system in which the Sanskrit language was considered to be the language of the Gods, the Deva Pasha, and for this reason, its use was restricted to the Brahmin caste. Using the language of the ordinary people, Guru Angad developed the Gurmukhi script which, by virtue of the fact that it was easy to read, helped to promote literacy among his followers. This allowed his message to spread more widely. He wrote down the hymns of Guru Nanak in Gurmukhi script and these formed the basis of the Sikh scriptures.

With the service and devotion of his wife, Mata Khivi, Guru Angad continued the institution of *langar*, the free kitchen for the poor, which Guru Nanak had initiated. Guru Angad chose his devoted disciple Amar Das as his successor.

Guru Amar Das, 1552–74

Guru Amar Das was the Sikh Guru during the reign of the Mughal Emperor Akbar (1542–1605). His many contributions to the development of the Sikh faith included the expansion of the *langar*, to both Sikhs and non-Sikhs. Those attending the *langar* were encouraged to participate in either preparing the food or cleaning once they had eaten. The Hindu caste structure prohibited social interaction between those of different castes. In particular, the high caste Brahmins were forbidden to invite those of a lower caste into their homes or to eat with them. The *langar* activity contributed to the disintegration of the caste system because all members of society, regardless of social rank, caste or creed, would sit side by side preparing food, eating and cleaning up together. Thus, in the Punjab, in places where the Sikh Gurus preached and where the *langar* kitchens were established, caste barriers were gradually being eroded.

Guru Amar Das was also responsible for a compilation of the writings of Guru Nanak, Guru Angad and some Hindu saints. This anthology is the basis of the present *Guru Granth Sahib*.

Guru Ram Das, 1574–81

Guru Ram Das was held in high esteem by the Emperor Akbar and, in 1577, Akbar made a land grant to the Guru. It was on this land that the Guru founded a settlement, dug a sacred pool and, later, began to build the Harimandir, the temple of God

Historical Context

Figure 1 Watercolour painting with a pen and ink border, showing the Harimandir Temple surrounded by the sacred pool in Amritsar. Company School, 19th century. British Museum, 1984,0124,0.1.17

(Fig. 1). This new town became Guru Ram Das' home and was known as Guru-ka-Chak or Ramdaspur. It soon developed into a regional commercial centre and was later renamed Amritsar to reflect the spiritual significance of the city.

Guru Arjan, 1581–1606

Guru Ram Das' third son succeeded him 1581. His first task was the completion of the city of Ramdaspur (Amritsar), the sacred pool and the Harimandir in the centre of the pool. In order to raise funds to complete the Harimandir in Amritsar, Guru Arjan introduced a system of taxation whereby each Sikh was asked to annually donate 1/10 of his income, the *daswandh* to the Guru. The Harimandir was successfully completed with these funds. Guru Arjan encouraged his disciples to participate in trade and commerce and, as traders settled in Amritsar, it flourished and became increasingly prosperous.

A significant development for the Sikh faith was the compilation of the Sikh holy book called the *Adi Granth*. Guru Arjan provided the Sikhs with an authoritative scripture by collating the hymns written by Guru Nanak and the succeeding Gurus into a single volume which became the core of the Sikh scriptures. This collection of hymns also included Guru Arjan's work. The creation of this unified scripture written in a new and more easily accessible script, Gurmukhi, gave the Sikhs a distinct cultural and religious identity. In August 1604 the sacred book was installed in the Harimandir in Amritsar.

The Sikh Gurus maintained peaceful relations with Akbar and he, in turn, appreciated their activities. However, after Akbar's death in 1605 the Sikhs faced great challenges under his successor Jahangir. During a rebellion by Jahanghir's son Khusru, Guru Arjan sided with the prince and was heavily fined as a consequence. The Guru denied the charge of treason and, for this reason, was arrested and imprisoned in Lahore. He was martyred in 1606 after being tortured.

Guru Hargobind, 1606–44

After the death of his father Guru Arjan in 1606, Guru Hargobind became the sixth Guru of the Sikhs. Under Jahangir's reign, Guru Arjan had anticipated further difficult times ahead for the Sikhs and had instructed Baba Budha, a respected and knowledgeable devotee of the Sikh Gurus, to train the young Hargobind in the art of warfare. Shortly before his death, Guru Arjan had informed the Sikhs that his son would become Guru and maintain an army to the best of his ability. From a young age, Guru Hargobind wore two swords to represent the balance of spiritual and temporal power.

Guru Hargobind followed his father's vision and created a Sikh army to defend the Sikh faith against the increasingly aggressive actions of the Mughal Emperors against their non-Muslim subjects.

He built a fort at Lohgarh and created the Akal Takht, the seat of temporal power, opposite the Harimandir in Amritsar. The Akal Takht later became the Sikh political centre. Guru Hargobind took part in a number of battles in the Punjab, beginning with the battle of Amritsar in 1634, and claimed several minor victories over local Mughal commanders.

The Guru nominated his grandson Guru Har Rai as the seventh Guru of the Sikhs before his death in 1644.

Guru Har Rai, 1644–61

Guru Har Rai became Guru at the age of 14. He continued his father's work and maintained a force of 2,000 armed Sikhs. The Guru was heavily involved in organisational and missionary work and died at the age of 32 in Kiratpur, Punjab in October 1661.

Guru Harkrishan, 1661–64

Guru Harkrishan, the younger son of Guru Har Rai, was recognised as the eighth Guru of the Sikhs in 1661. He was called a 'child saint' because he was only six years of age when he became Guru and died within a few years of small-pox in 1664. Before his death he announced that his successor would be found in the village of Baba Bakala near Goindwal, Amritsar.

Guru Tegh Bahadur, 1664–75

Tegh Bahadur, the son of Guru Hargobind, became Guru in 1664 at the age of 43. He founded a new settlement in the Punjab which later grew into the town of Anandpur. The Emperor Aurangzeb considered the Sikhs and Hindus to be infidels and, therefore, ordered the destruction of all Sikh and Hindu temples and the defilement of their religious teachings and practices. During this violence, many Hindu Pundits from Kashmir were forcibly converted to Islam. They approached Guru Tegh Bahadur for help and the Guru took up their cause as he believed in religious freedom. When the Emperor heard about this, the Guru was summoned to the Mughal court in Delhi. On his way there, he and his companions were arrested and, on the following day, the Guru was beheaded at Chandani Chowk, Delhi on 11 November 1675. A devoted follower of the Guru took his head to Gobind Singh, the son of the Guru.

Guru Gobind Singh, 1675–1708

Guru Gobind Singh, the only child of Guru Tegh Bahadur, was born in Patna in 1666. After his father's execution in 1675, he became the 10th Guru of the Sikhs at the age of nine. His education encompassed the study of both intellectual and military arts. In 1678 Guru Gobind Singh settled in Anandpur and confirmed that this strategic site would be his base.

The increasing tyranny of the Mughal rulers led Guru Gobind Singh to militarise the Sikhs and create the *Khalsa*, a military order of Sikhs. In 1699 all male Sikhs were given the name *Singh*, 'lion', and females were given the name *Kaur* meaning 'princess'. Men and women were baptised into the Sikh faith by drinking water sweetened with sugar crystals and churned by the *Khanda*, double-edged sword. This event occurred in the month of *Vaisakh*[6] and, for this reason, is known as Vaisakhi. With the formation of the *Khalsa*, Guru Gobind Singh established unity, cohesion and organisation for the Sikh people. The Sikh army would defend those individuals who were suffering from persecution under the Mughal government.

The Guru and his Sikh army won numerous battles against opposing forces, such as the Hindu Hill Rajas who wanted to take over the Punjab. Aurangzeb further antagonized the Sikhs by ordering the death of Guru Gobind Singh's youngest sons by walling them up alive. On hearing the news of the death of his sons, Guru Gobind Singh wrote a letter, the *Zafarnama*, to Aurangzeb rebuking him for his actions. With a few of his followers, Guru Gobind Singh moved towards the Deccan via Rajasthan to the town of Nanded. In Nanded the Guru met a man who became an ardent disciple of his and was later named Banda Bahadur. The Guru chose him as the commander of the Sikh forces and instructed him to go the Punjab and keep the Mughal forces at bay.

Shortly after this, Banda travelled to the Punjab and the Guru was attacked by hired assassins. Guru Gobind Singh was severely injured and died in 1708.

Before he died, Guru Gobind Singh declared that the *Guru Granth Sahib* (Holy book) would be the future and eternal Guru of the Sikhs hereafter. The *Guru Granth Sahib* contains the compilation of the scriptures written by the previous Gurus and holy Hindu and Muslim saints.

The Khalsa Republic

Banda Singh Bahadur, 1710–16

Shortly before his death in 1708, Guru Gobind Singh appointed Banda Singh Bahudur, leader of the Sikhs. Banda Singh Bahadur was given 25 soldiers and an advisory council of five trusted Sikhs. As Banda Singh Bahadur reached the Punjab, many Sikhs began to join his army.

In 1710 a battle was fought at Chapar Chiri near Sirhind, where Banda Bahadur defeated and killed Wazir Khan the Mughal governor of Sirhind. Consequently, the Sikhs took over Sirhind and established themselves at Mukhlispur, north-east of Ambala. Here, Banda Bahadur repaired an existing fortress and renamed it Lohgarh.

It is believed that the first Sikh coin was minted at the Lohgarh fort shortly after the occupation of this area. For some months, Banda Singh Bahadur gained notable successes against the Mughals and controlled most of the region between Delhi and the river Ravi.

Following the death of the Mughal Emperor Shah 'Alam Bahadur, the Sikhs were able to regain large parts of the Punjab. Banda Singh Bahadur abolished the Mughal Zaminidari system[7] under which aristocrats ruled over the peasants living and working on the land. Instead, Banda Singh Bahadur declared that the cultivators were the owners of the land that they worked. His leadership indicated the beginnings of a Sikh state, giving hope of a more just and fair system for Sikhs.

In 1716 Furrukhsiyar, Mughal Emperor between the years 1713–19, appointed the general 'Abd as-Samand Khan Diler Jang as the governor of Lahore. This event led to the end of Banda Singh Bahadur's rule. In response to Banda's actions, his abolishment of existing systems, the Mughal governor killed thousands of Sikhs in the Punjab and sent others to Delhi where they were tortured and killed. Banda Bahadur and his infant son were themselves executed in June 1716.

Although Banda Singh's uprising against the Mughal government was very brief, it was nonetheless a critical event in the formation of the forthcoming Sikh Misal period and crucial for the ultimate establishment of the Sikh Empire.

The Sikh Misals, 1760–1801

Following Banda Singh Bahadur's death in 1716, the Sikhs remained militarily inactive until the latter half of the 18th century. They were one of four powers competing for the possession of the Punjab. These included the Mughals, the Afghan Durranis and the Marathas. Under the pressure of Ahmad Shah Durrani's repeated invasions, the Mughal Empire centred in Delhi rapidly collapsed and the regions of Lahore, Multan, Sind, Sirhind and Kashmir became part of the Durrani dominions.

The Sikh Misals, or 'confederacies', took advantage of the declining Mughal Empire and the persistence of the Afghan invaders to form a strong army. Ahmad Shah Durrani invaded the Punjab on several occasions between the years 1751 and 1770 and desecrated the temple at Amritsar on at least two occasions by filling the sacred pool with mud and dirt. After these hardships the Sikhs decided to form a defensive body and collectively called themselves the *Dal Khalsa* meaning army of the *Khalsa*. By uniting as a force in this way, they managed to

Map 1 The Territories of the Sikh Misals 1760–1801

increase their power and triumphed over the great Afghan leader.

The Sikh Misals gained possession of the Punjab through a system called *Rakhi*, 'protection'. The Sikhs provided protection to the people against foreign invaders, local landowners and government officials. Due to the extensive territories that required protection, the Sikhs found it necessary to divide themselves into different units, thereby organizing themselves into a form of government known as the Misals.

The Misals consisted of 12 separate divisions that conquered their own territories (**Map 1**), while uniting themselves in a single Sikh army the 'Dal Khalsa'. Each Misal followed a leader or *Sardar*, 'chieftain' (**Table 1**).

Displaying their loyalty to the principles of the 10th Guru, Guru Gobind Singh, the Misals engaged in the spirit of the *Khalsa*. A common treasury and the free kitchen, or *langar* as mentioned on page 2, instigated mutual cooperation amongst the different groups. The Misals ruled in the name of the Guru and the *Khalsa*. Any victory over the enemy was not considered the triumph of an individual leader but, rather, one of the Sikh commonwealth.

The Misals operated in a distinctive way because there was no one specific leader. Despite the absence of a single leader, the governing of the state remained efficient and successful. The *Sarbat Khalsa*, entire body of Sikhs, met twice a year at Amritsar on the Vaisakhi and Diwali festivals. At these meetings the Sikh chiefs would pass a *gurmatta* which was a formal decision or resolution made before the *Guru Granth Sahib*. As their meetings were held in the presence of the Guru, the Misals strongly believed that the decisions made were representative of the Guru's will. The *gurmatta* system demonstrated the strength and unity of the *Khalsa*.

Table 1: The 12 Sikh Misals

Misal	Area of control
Ahluwalia Misal	Kapurthala
Bhangi Misal	Amritsar
Ramgarhia Misal	Sri Hargobindpur
Faizullapuria Misal	Jalandhar
Sukerchakia Misal	Gujranwala
Karorsinghia Misal	Bunga
Nishanwalia Misal	Ambala
Dallewalia Misal	Rahon
Phulkia Misal	Patiala, Nabha
Nakai Misal	Chunian
Shaheedan Misal	Shazadpur
Khanaya Misal	Fathepur

On 17 April 1765, the Sikh chiefs occupied the fort of Lahore. After holding an assembly at Amritsar, the Sikh Misals declared their independence and struck a coin in the name of the Sikh Gurus to represent their conquest and their faith. Silver rupees were issued in Lahore in 1765 followed by the minting of coins in Amritsar in 1775.

Although the Misals were united in their aims, the problem of undefined boundaries between their lands and the ownership of their possessions often caused disruption to their mutual relations. The desire to extend individual boundaries and create new territories led to rivalries between the Misal leaders. This inter-group competition was problematic because it caused the Misals to act independently of one another in addition to fighting as a collective force.

The Sikh Empire, 1801–49

Maharaja Ranjit Singh, 1780–1839

Ranjit Singh (**Fig. 2**) was the son of Sardar Mahan Singh, leader of the Sukerchakia Misal, and succeeded his father in this post. He became a great king and leader of the Sikhs, expanding territories and uniting the people to form what was known as the 'Sikh Empire'.

The political unity of the Punjab had once again weakened for two main reasons. Firstly, infighting, between the Misals and, secondly, Zaman Shah, the grandson of Ahmad Shah Durrani, was threatening an invasion. Rivalry between the Misal leaders was at its height and the Punjab had been divided into several principalities. In 1798 Zaman Shah's army marched to the Punjab and made an attempt to occupy Lahore. Ranjit Singh prevented the Afghans from succeeding and forced them to retreat to the surrounding countryside. Ranjit Singh himself occupied Lahore in 1799 at the age of 19 with the assistance of his mother-in-law, Sada Kaur. With Ranjit Singh's decisive actions, the Sukerchakia Misal became more successful and increased in power which in turn resulted in the consolidation of the Punjab.

The Sikh Misals united under Ranjit Singh's leadership to form a defence force against the surrounding enemies. The leaders of each Misal were given high ministerial and military positions alongside Hindu counsellors and Muslim princes at Ranjit Singh's court and European soldiers were soon attracted here as well.

According to Ganda Singh in *A Life Sketch of the Maharaja*, chiefs and prominent notables offered the title *Maharaja*, 'great king' to Ranjit Singh on the day of Vaisakhi in 1801. However, Bhagat Singh claims that on that day a grand *durbar* (meaning court) was organised where Ranjit Singh assumed the title of *Sarkar*, 'leader' and not that of *Maharaja*.[8]

Although his subjects referred to him as *Maharaja* and to some extent he fulfilled the role of a royal king, Ranjit Singh believed that he was a humble servant of God, dedicated to the service of the people.

Despite facing hostility from the Afghans and the Marathas, Ranjit Singh created a large state and established an efficient administration. Annexing the vast territories of the Misal confederacies, Ranjit Singh rapidly expanded his possessions to include the areas of Amritsar, Jullandhar and Gurdaspur. He continued to issue Sikh coins from Lahore and Amritsar and the mints were under his direct control (see map, right).

During the first decade of his rule, Ranjit Singh brought the Sikh Misal leaders under his overall authority and during the second decade of his rule, he occupied the entire trans-Sutlej[9] territories of the Punjab including, Kashmir, Jammum Peshawar and Derajat.[9] Ranjit Singh had formed a powerful and prosperous kingdom and had fulfilled his ambition of raising a great Sikh Empire. By 1820, it can be said that the power of Ranjit Singh was absolute throughout the whole of the Punjab which stretched from the Sutlej to the Indus (**Map 2**).

Ranjit Singh had good relations with the British in India because the Punjab formed a geographical buffer against the increasing threat of the Afghan and Russian forces. In 1809 he signed the Treaty of Amritsar with Charles T. Metcalfe who represented the British East India Company, by which terms he renounced his supremacy over the cis-sutlej[9] chiefs and British occupation was limited to the regions south of the river Sutlej.

Ranjit Singh maintained good relations with the British for the rest of his reign.

Figure 2 Watercolour painting with a pen and ink border, showing Ranjit Singh, ruler of the Sikh Empire. Company School, 19th century. British Museum, 1984,0124,0.1.17

Map 2 The Empire of Ranjit Singh 1839

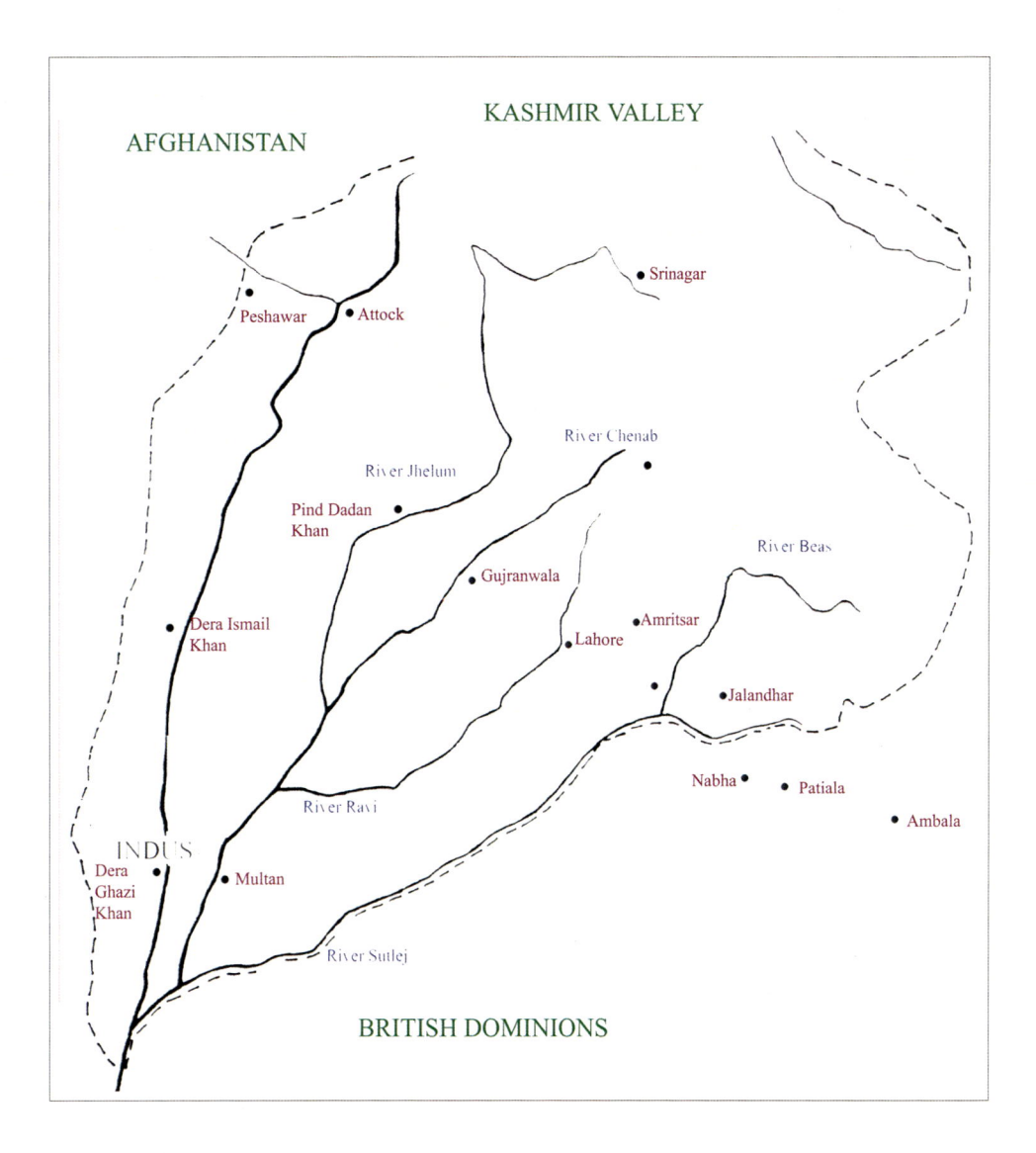

The Sikh Empire began to decline rapidly after Ranjit Singh's death in 1839.

Kharak Singh (**Fig. 3**), the eldest son of Ranjit Singh, was acknowledged as the ruler of the Punjab but he failed to maintain his father's legacy and died at the age of 38. Both Nau-Nihal Singh (**Fig. 4**), Kharak Singh's son, and Sher Singh (**Fig. 5**), Ranjit Singh's illegitimate son, were killed by potential usurpers to the throne. The lack of a single, central authority left the kingdom open to invasion.

In the latter half of 1845 the British East India Company had strengthened its military power by setting up a military cantonment at Ferozepur, close to the river Sutlej, and having annexed Sindh in the south of the Punjab. According to J.D. Cunningham, the Company's main concern was that the Khalsa army without a strong leadership was a serious threat to British territories along the border.[10] The Punjab would also no longer be able to act as a buffer zone between the Company's possessions in India and Afghanistan. This increase in British military strength led to tension with the Sikh forces and in November 1845 the Sikhs crossed the territories of their allies infringing the terms of the 1809 treaty. This in turn led to the advance of British troops towards the Sutlej and onto Sikh territory on 11 December 1845 resulting in the first Anglo-Sikh War.

Figure 3 Portrait of Maharaja Kharak Singh (ruled 1839–40), eldest son of Ranjit Singh. Painited on paper, Pahari School, c. 1850. British Museum, 1937,0312,0.2

Further battles took place between the Sikhs and the British in the following years, with the Punjab finally falling into the hands of the British and its annexation in 1849. Ranjit Singh's youngest son, Dulip Singh (**Fig. 6**), was exiled to Britain shortly after the annexation of the Punjab.

A table detailing the reigns of Mughal, Sikh and Afghan rulers can be found in Appendix 1.

Notes
1. 'Khatri' is the Punjabi equivalent for the Sanskrit *Kshatriya*. It is the Hindu warrior caste.
2. Muslim landlord of the village.
3. Singh, K. 2004, 67.
4. *Modikhana* is a Persian word for the place where grain is stored, before being distributed as required.
5. Singh, K. 2004, 63.
6. The *Guru Granth Sahib* is the compilation of Sikh scriptures written by the Sikh Gurus and holy saints, it is the final and eternal Guru of the Sikhs.
7. A system similar to feudalism in medieval Europe.
8. Singh, B. 1993, 196.
9. Trans-Sutlej meaning the region north of the river Sutlej. Cis-Sutlej refers to those south of the river Sutlej.
10. Cunningham, 1915, 258.

Figure 4 Portrait of Nau-Nihal Singh, son of Kharak Singh. Painted on paper, Pahari School, c. 1850. British Museum, 1937,0312,0.3

Figure 5 Watercolour painting with a pen and ink border showing Sher Singh (ruled 1840–43 AD), illegitimate son of Ranjit Singh. Company School, 19th century. British Museum, 1984,0124,0.1.4

Figure 6 Watercolour painting with a pen and ink border, showing Dulip Singh, Ranjit Singh's youngest son. Company School, 19th century. British Museum, 1984,0124,0.1.2

Chapter 2
Sikh Mints

The Sikhs began to produce coins in the traditional mint centres (**Map 3**) once Mughal power had started to decline and the Afghans had left the Punjab.

Lahore had been a mint under the authority of both the Mughal Empire and the Durrani dynasty. The first Sikh coin was struck in Lahore in 1765. The city of Multan also had a functioning mint that continued to be used by the Sikh Misals and coins were minted there until the end of Sikh rule. With the expansion of the Sikh kingdom in the 19th century, Sikh mints were also established at Amritsar, Peshawar, Kashmir and Derajat.

Important information about these Punjabi cities when the Sikhs were in power was recorded by Charles Masson, explorer, archaeologist and numismatist.

Having deserted the East India Company's army, Masson (real name James Lewis), wandered through Sind, Baluchistan, Afghanistan the Punjab during the period 1826–40. During these years he explored places that were little, if at all, known to the world at large, for example Kabul, Ghazni and Kandahar. Masson recorded his travels in his three-volume work *Narratives of Various Journeys in Balochistan, Afghanistan and the Punjab*. After spending nearly two years in Afghanistan, he spent the following year moving between Sind and the Punjab.

The time Masson spent in the Punjab includes the period under discussion in this catalogue, specifically the reign of Ranjit Singh (1801–39). Masson gives descriptive accounts of cities that he visited in the Punjab, including Amritsar, Lahore and Multan. In Lahore, he was warmly received by Jean

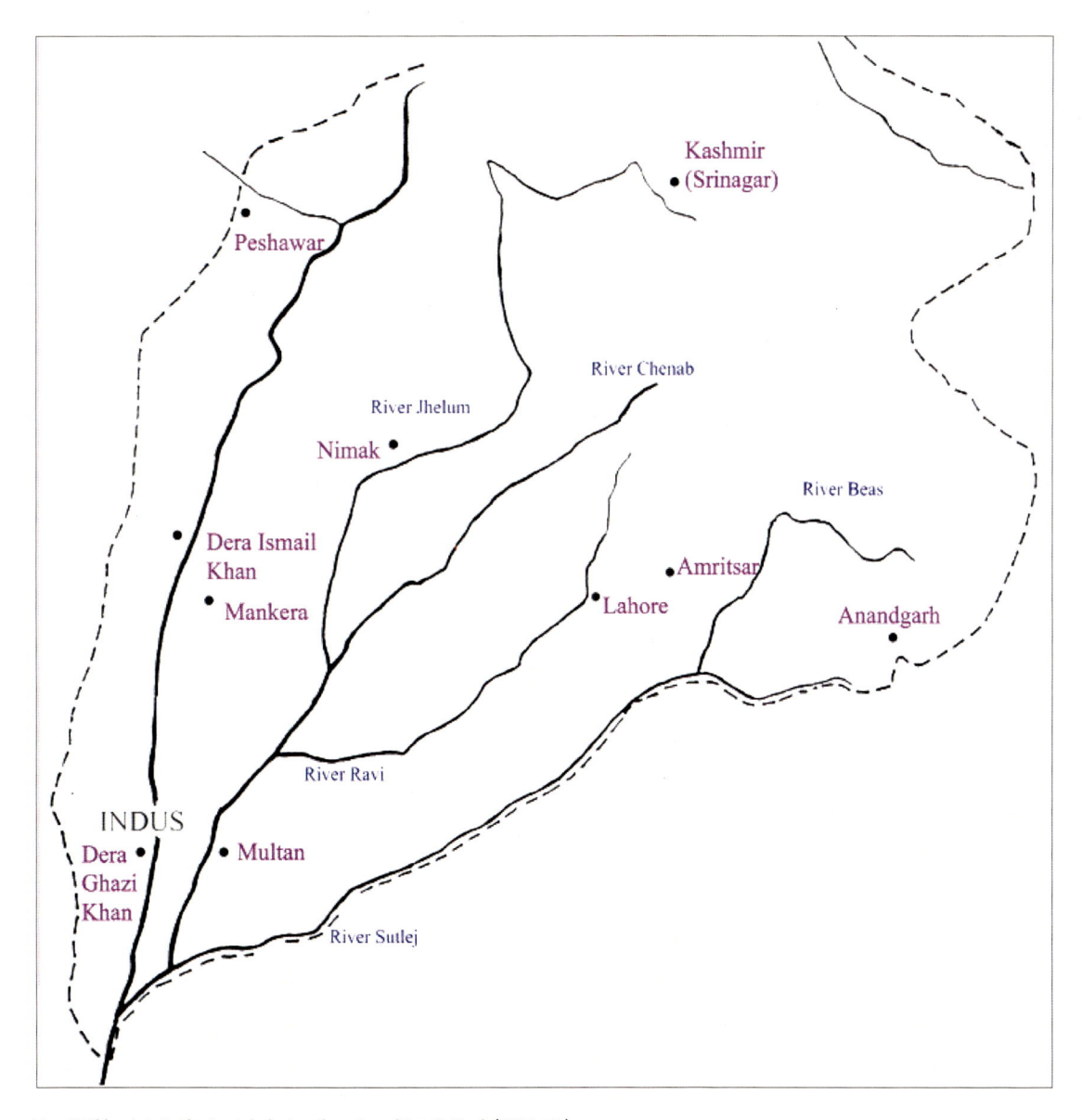

Map 3 Sikh mints in the Punjab during the reign of Ranjit Singh (1801–39)

Francois Allard, Ranjit Singh's French general. He left Lahore after a short stay to avoid entering the Sikh military service and made his way to Peshawar. From Peshawar he went through Faizilpur and Shikarpur and entered lower Sind. Masson's accounts provide unique socioeconomic information for the Punjab during the Sikh Empire, not least because he visited the majority of the cities where the Sikh mints were established.[1] Some of Masson's descriptions are quoted below.

Amritsar

Amritsar, the holy city and spiritual centre of the Sikhs, was founded by Guru Ram Das, the fourth Sikh Guru (1534–81), who had obtained the land from the Mughal Emperor Akbar.

In the city, which was originally known as Ramdaspur, a sacred pool was dug and later the Harimandir was completed by Guru Arjun Dev, the fifth Guru.[2] The city was later named Amritsar, 'pool of immortality'. Amrit meaning the 'ambrosial nectar' and Sar meaning 'pool or fountain'. After the Harimandir was completed, the city of Amritsar became the Sikh spiritual centre and increasing numbers of pilgrims were drawn to it.

In 1608, the sixth Guru, Guru Hargobind, built the Akal Takht, 'seat of the Immortal', a building which represented the political authority of the Sikhs in Amritsar close to the Harimandir temple.

During the 18th century, the Afghan armies attempted to destroy the temple and defile the sacred tank on several occasions. By 1767, however, the Afghans no longer posed a threat and the Sikh Misals established themselves in the city. Amritsar was now under the control of the Bhangi Misal which was made up of approximately 10 different families, each of whom controlled different parts of the city and built small forts around the area.[3] At the turn of the 18th century, Amritsar had become part of Maharaja Ranjit Singh's expanding empire and was the centre of trade activity in the Punjab. Recognised as the commercial emporium of northern India, goods were imported from Central Asia and India, while exports from the city included grain, sugar, rice, silk shawls and gold and silver articles.

In the late 1820s, Charles Masson wrote:

> Lahore, although possessing a certain degree of trade and traffic with its populous vicinity, is a dull city, in a commercial sense. Amritsar has become the great mart of the Punjab, and the bankers and capitalists of the country have taken up their abodes there.[4]

According to Herrli,[5] the average annual output of coins from the Amritsar mint was approximately 1 million rupees, making the city a financial centre and the chief mint for rupees and copper coins.[6]

The rupees issued from the mint during Ranjit Singh's reign display varying mint marks in any given year. A possible explanation for this could be that Amritsar had one chief mint with several smaller workshops using a different set of mint marks.

It is possible that there was more than one mint operating in Amritsar and it is assumed that there was a central administration responsible for controlling the striking and issuing of the coins. There is, however, only limited literary evidence in support of this claim.

See Appendix 2 for a table depicting the different mints' markings.

Anandgarh

The village of Anandpur, 'haven of rest', was founded by the ninth Sikh Guru, Guru Tegh Bahadur, in 1665. The Guru paid 500 rupees for the land which had been offered to him by the Dowager Queen Champa of Bilaspur. Anandpur is located on the lower spurs of the Himalayas and falls within the modern district of Rupnagar in India.

The 10th Guru, Guru Gobind Singh, made Anandpur his stronghold and built several forts in the area. The main fort was named Anandgarh and it is possible that coins were minted here in the late 18th century.

Only rupees have been noted from this mint and they are scarce in comparison with coins produced by other Sikh mints. There are only four rupees from this mint in the British Museum collection and these were produced in the years 1784, 1785, 1786 and 1787.

Herrli suggests that the coins displaying the Anandgarh mint name were most probably struck in Amritsar because they bear a strong resemblance to a series of the Amritsar Gobindshahi rupees. According to Herrli, the fortress built by Guru Gobind Singh at Anandpur never had a mint for coining rupees. He writes 'The Gobindshahis of Amritsar and Anandgarh are very similar and differ only in respective reverse designs; the mint name, the mark and an unexplained era year.'[7]

It remains uncertain whether these coins were minted in the fort of Anandgarh in Anandpur because there is no literary evidence to conclusively confirm or deny that a functioning mint existed in this region.

Lahore

Lahore has been a prominent city since the time of the Mughal Empire. Under Babur the first Mughal emperor (1526–30), coins were first minted in Lahore and they continued to be minted by his grandson Akbar and, thereafter, by the successive rulers up to, and including, Mughual ruler Alamgir II (1754–59).

During the 18th century, Ahmad Shah Durrani made several attempts to occupy Lahore and drive away Maratha power. However, during a brief return to Kabul, Jassa Singh Ahluwalia and the Sikhs took over the city.[8] The Durranis' hold on the Punjab weakened as the power of the Sikhs continued to increase and, on 17 April 1765, the Sikhs had complete control over the fort of Lahore.

In 1793 Zaman Shah succeeded as the leader of the Durrani dynasty and invaded Lahore in 1797 with little opposition. After briefly occupying the city, he was called back to Afghanistan to deal with an internal dispute. He renewed his invasion the following year but was unable to gain long-term control of the city. After Zaman Shah was recalled to Afghanistan, Lahore was left to the Sikhs and Ranjit Singh gained overall control and declared himself Maharaja of Lahore. The city was to remain the political capital of the Sikh kingdom until it was annexed by the British in 1849.

Although the Sikhs occupied Lahore intermittently, they were eager to strike coins as soon as they had the opportunity. The first Sikh rupee was minted at Lahore in 1765 during their initial invasion. The rupees followed the weight standards of regular Mughal and Durrani coinage. Zaman Shah Durrani's temporary control of Lahore between 1797 and 1798 did not appear to disrupt the minting of the Sikh coins.

The mint in Lahore was situated outside the Taxsali, 'mint' gate south of the Badshahi mosque in the old walled city. According to a British report of 1846, the mint had the capacity to produce up to 8,000 coins per day.[9]

Like the nearby city Amritsar, Lahore was a bustling trading centre specialising in the trade of cotton cloth, silk, shawls and arms. Lahore, the capital of the Sikh State, was also the main residence of the Maharaja and his family. Masson wrote,

> Lahore, the capital of the Punjab and of the territories of Ranjit Singh, is a city of undoubted antiquity, and has long been celebrated for its extent and magnificence.
>
> To it also must be referred the current proverb, which asserts that Isfahan and Shiraz united would not equal half of Lahore.[10]

Multan

Multan was located approximately 6km away from the left bank of the river Chenab and close to the old bed of the river Ravi. It was ruled by the Sikhs during two phases of occupation.

First Sikh occupation: 1772–79

Shortly after Ahmad Shah Durrani's final invasion of the city, the Sikhs conquered the Multan province led by Jhanda Singh, leader of the Bhangi Misal, in 1767. The Sikhs also attempted to attack the provincial capital but the joint forces of the Afghan governor and the Daudputras (neighbouring rulers) of Bahawalpur put up a strong resistance. Later, an internal quarrel among these opposing forces provided the Sikh troops with an opportunity to invade and, in December 1772, Jhanda Singh took over the citadel of the city and also the fort and town of Mankera.[11]

For several years, Multan remained under the authority of the Bhangi Misal who continued to collect taxes from the local landowners.

In 1777 and 1778, the son of Ahmad Shah, Taimur Shah Durrani, unsuccessfully attempted to recapture the city. In 1779, Timur Shah decided to personally lead his troops into Multan and, after limited resistance, the Sikhs surrendered the citadel to the Afghan leader.

Second Sikh occupation: 1818–48

Beginning in 1802, Ranjit Singh made a number of attempts to bring Multan under the authority of the Sikh realm. In 1817, he finally accepted funds from Muzaffar Khan, which had been repeatedly offered to him over the years to withdraw his forces.[12]

In June 1818 the Sikhs entered the city yet again and this time, the attack was unexpected. The Afghans were unable to resist this advance and the Sikhs were able to capture the citadel. After this, Multan remained part of the Sikh kingdom until 1848. Coins were minted in Multan during the two Sikh occupations: 1772–79 and 1818–48.

In 1821 Ranjit Singh appointed Sawan Mal, one of his administrators, as governor of the Multan province, a role that he performed successfully for almost a quarter of a century.

The city of Multan was also commercially and financially prosperous. Masson wrote:

> Multan is said to have decreased in trade since it fell into the hands of the Sikhs, yet its bazaars continued well and are reasonably supplied with all articles of traffic and consumption. There are still numerous bankers and manufacturers of silk and cotton goods.'
>
> It still supplies a portion of its fabrics to the Lohani merchants of Afghanistan, and has an extensive foreign trade with the regions west of the Indus.[13]

Multan was stormed by British troops in 1849 and after this it formed part of the British Empire. Small gold coins were found by those British troops who occupied the citadel. It is believed that these emergency gold rupees were issued by the governor of Multan, Diwan Mulraj, to pay his troops between 1848 and 1849. As Diwan Mulraj was short of silver, he coined a hoard of gold worth 40 lakh rupees into small pieces that passed for 1 rupee each.[14] See Chapter 3 for denominations and circulation of Sikh currency.

Kashmir

Kashmir had been under the control of the Afghan Durrani dynasty for 70 years until 1819 when the Kashmiris sought external help to relieve them from Afghan rule. Diwan Chand, one of Ranjit Singh's trusted and capable generals led an army into Kashmir in April 1819. The Sikhs were faced with little opposition because the majority of Afghan troops which had been stationed in Kashmir were attending to matters in Kabul. By July 1819 the Sikhs had occupied Srinagar, the capital of Kashmir.

Once the capital city of Kashmir was taken, Ranjit Singh gave Misr Diwan Chand the title of 'Zafar Jang' meaning 'victorious in battle'. The Sikhs ruled Kashmir for 27 years and 12 different governors were employed by the Maharaja to administer the city over the course of these years.

Srinagar was a successful manufacturing and financial centre. Many goods, including arms, jewellery, leather and saffron, were exported to the Punjab, Sind, Ladakh and Tibet. It was most famous for its production of Kashmiri shawls which were exported to Central Asia, Russia, China and Europe. This trade generated an impressive income which ensured the economic stability of the city.

The Kashmir mint was supervised by whichever governor was in post and his main responsibilities included economic and monetary policy. The Sikh coins of Kashmir bear a special mark representing the authority of the governor who was in charge of the territory at the time of production (**Table 2**).

Derajat

Derajat is the collective name given to the three Deras 'settlements' on the plain between the river Indus in the east and with the Suliaman mountain range to the west. Dera Ismail Khan is located in the north of this region, Dera Ghazi Khan to the south and Dera Fath Khan is in the centre. Although these settlements were founded in the late 15th century, they only gained importance after the invasion of Nadir Shah in 1738–39.

Dera Fath Khan was a functioning mint under Nadir Shah issuing mostly autonomous copper coinage. Dera Ghazi Khan was a prominent mint for the Afghan Durrani Shahs. In 1820 both of these settlements fell to Sikh occupation.

Table 2: Governors of Kashmir and the symbols on their coins

Governor	Symbol
Diwan Chand Governor of Kashmir until the end of 1819.	No symbol
Diwan Moti Ram Son of a well known minister of Ranjit Singh. He succeeded Misr Diwan Chand at the end of 1819 and governed until early 1820.	No symbol
Sardar Hari Singh Nalwa Ranjit Singh's general. He won fame during the conquests of Multan, Peshawar and Kashmir. He is said to have introduced a new rupee of base coinage in Kashmir. He was governor from early in 1820 until the end of 1821.	No symbol
Diwan Moti Ram Reappointed governor for a second term and served as such throughout 1822 until the end of 1824.	No symbol
Diwan Chuni Lal Hindu governor of Kashmir for two years: throughout 1825 and 1826. On being recalled to Lahore for misgovernment, he committed suicide on route there.	No symbol
Diwan Kirpa Ram Son of Moti Ram. Appears to have been appointed governor at the end of 1826, holding office for three years and ten months. Recalled suddenly to Lahore during the summer of 1831.	ک
Bhima Singh Ardali Held office as a temporary measure for approximately 12 months from the middle of 1831.	ب ਗ
Sher Singh Reputed to have been son of Ranjit Singh. Governor of Kashmir from 1832 until 1834.	↑
Colonel Mehan Singh Kumedan Governor from 1834 until 1841; also Commandant of the Sikh garrison there. Seems to have been the best of the Sikh administrators, doing much to restore trade, industry and agriculture in the valley. His term in office was probably extended by Ranjit Singh's death in 1839. Killed by rebellious soldiers on 17 April 1841.	◡
Shaikh Gholam Muhyid Din First Muslim governor of Kashmir. Had been chief Munsi (clerk) to Moti Ram but was dismissed when Hari Singh took office. Supported himself as a Munsi until Karak Singh became Maharajah of Punjab. His abilities then seem to have been recognised and he was appointed governor, holding this position until 1845.	ن
Shaikh Imam ud Din Son of Gholam Muhyid Din. Held the office of governor until November 1846 when Gulab Singh of Jammu took possession of Kashmir.	ن

'Dera Ismail Khan', referred to as 'Derajat', produced coins under the Mughal emperors Muhammad Shah and Ahmad Shah Bahadur (1719–54) and then briefly under Nadir Shah and continued minting under the Durrani Shahs until 1818.' After Mahmud Shah Durrani's second reign (1809–18), he was deposed by the Barakzais.[16] However, he continued to rule in Herat from 1818 until his death in 1829. In 1820 Ranjit Singh took over the fortress of Mankera and controlled the surrounding area. The authority of the Sikhs in Dera Ismail Khan did not disrupt the production of rupees bearing Mahmud Shah Durrani's name. Coins minted after his death in 1829 were considered to be posthumous issues in tribute to the Sikhs.

The first official Sikh coin was minted at Derajat in 1835 when Ranjit Singh conquered the area and it officially became part of the Sikh Empire. The coins replaced those of Mahmud Shah Durrani and were produced on small thick flans with only partially visible inscriptions.

Derajat had approximately 450,000 inhabitants when under Sikh rule and had become a thriving trading centre.

> Dera Ismail Khan is one of the greatest marts on the Indus, an entrepot for the merchandize of India and Khorasan passing in this direction. Few sites have a greater commercial importance.[17]

Peshawar

The town of Peshawar was given its name, which means 'frontier town', by the Mughal Emperor Akbar (1556–1605). Peshawar was invaded and briefly ruled by Nadir Shah before it became an official mint under the Durrani rulers. The Durranis issued coins from Peshawar from the time of Ahmad Shah to the reign of Ayub Shah (1819–23).

In 1818 Ranjit Singh briefly occupied the territory and again unsuccessfully attempted to exert his control in 1823. It was a decade later in 1834 when a Sikh army led by Nau Nihal Singh, grandson of Ranjit Singh, that the city was officially annexed and brought under the authority of the Sikh Empire.

The administration of the town depended on the taxation of the inhabitants. According to the fertility of the land, the Sikh government received either an eighth or a quarter of the produce.[18] As much of the land belonged to Ranjit Singh, the residents of Peshawar did not consider themselves independent.[19] Author Mohan Lal Esquire wrote:

> Such attention has been paid to agriculture and the amelioration of the soil, that no part of the Punjab country can equal the cultivated districts of Peshawar in beautiful scenery. It is certain that no city in the Punjab equals Peshawar in the richness of its soil. Grapes, figs, pomegranates, pears, apples, melons, oranges, peaches etc. are produced here.[20]

Later in 1834 Ranjit Singh appointed Sardar Hari Singh Nalwa as governor of Peshawar and the commander of a garrison of 12,000 men. Hari Singh Nalwa was granted the right to issue his own coins in return for his outstanding military achievements. The Peshawar coins date from 1834–37 and are of an outstanding quality in terms of calligraphy and die cutting. They bear the full Vikrama Samvat (vs) date on the obverse and the reverse, and do not mention Hari Singh by either a discreet or obvious means. Hari Singh died in 1837 and the production of the silver rupees ceased after this event.

Vikrama Samvat dates will be discussed in Chapter 5; there is a vs/AD conversion chart in Appendix 4.

Miscellaneous mints

Mankera

Mankera is located south-east of Dera Ismail Khan and approximately 130km north of Multan. The town was first occupied by the Sikhs in 1772 under the Bhangi Misal but was soon re- occupied by Taimur Shah Durrani in 1780. In 1821 Ranjit Singh personally led troops to Mankera and claimed it as part of his empire. The fort was strategically located between the rivers Indus and Chenab and controlled the road leading from Afghanistan through the Gomal-Pass and Dera Ismail Khan to Lahore. After annexing the cities of Mankera and Peshawar, Maharaja Ranjit Singh took control of the prominent routes between the Punjab and Afghanistan including the tribal territories of Kohat, Bannu and Waziristan.

There is limited literary evidence describing the city of Mankera as an operating mint.[21] However, the coin in the British Museum collection (1936,1017.42) dated vs 1879/ AD 1822, although quite worn, reveals part of this mint name on the reverse of the coin.

The Salt Range or 'Pind Dadan Khan' or 'Nimak'

In 1847 a mint was established in Pind Dadan Khan, a town at the foot of the Salt Range on the river Jhelum. It is claimed that Ranjit Singh had occupied this area at the end of the 18th century and that it operated as a mint for a short period between 1847 and 1848.[22]

Two coins in the British Museum collection have the word *nimak* as the mint name on the reverse.[23] *Nimak* means 'salt' in Persian, Urdu and Punjabi and may refer to the main commercial produce of the region rather than the actual minting place, suggesting that rupees minted in Pind Dadan Khan did not state the actual place of production.

Coins from this mint are very rare, and it remains unknown why they were struck for only a short period.

Notes

1. For more information on Charles Masson see Whitteridge, 1986. Masson also collected an extensive amount of coins and archaeological material, which he documented; in recent years this material has been the focus of a project at the British Museum, under the direction of Elizabeth Errington, and is now available on the Museum's website: http://www.britishmuseum.org/research/search_the_collection_database.aspx.
2. Also known as the Golden Temple, a name that was used after Ranjit Singh gilded the top of the temple.
3. Bhangi Misal was one of the 12 confederates governing the Punjab. It was founded by Chajja Singh during the mid-18th century.
4. Masson, 1974, 416.
5. Herrli, 2004, 43.
6. *Ibid.*
7. *Ibid,* 100.
8. Jassa Singh Ahluwalia was the leader of the Ahluwalia Misal.
9. Herrli, 2004, 169.
10. Masson, 1974, 408.
11. 130km north of Multan.
12. Governor of Multan, employed by Taimur Shah Durrani.
13. Masson, 1974, 395.
14. Herrli, 2004, 200.
15. Goran and Wiggins, 1983, 2.
16. Afghan dynasty ruled from 1826–1929.
17. Masson, 1974, 39.
18. Herrli, 2004, 211.
19. Masson, 1974, 126–35.
20. Lal, 1986.
21. Herrli, 2004, 203–5.
22. Rai, 1995, 13–15.
23. These have the registration numbers 1912,0709.301 and 1936,1017.39.

Chapter 3
Denominations and Circulation

During the Sikh Misal period, Sikh rupees followed the regular weight standards of Mughal and Durrani coinage, during which time a silver rupee weighed approximately 11.3g.[1]

Maharaja Ranjit Singh later expanded the monetary system in the Sikh Empire so that it comprised gold mohurs, silver rupees and copper paisas. Gold mohurs were issued in small numbers for use on special occasions, when they were given as *nazranas*, 'gifts'. The silver coins formed the basis of the Sikh coinage and were minted in three denominations: 1 rupee, 1/2 rupee and 1/4 rupee. The silver rupee weighed between 10.7 and 11.1g, and had a high silver purity. The copper coins comprised 1 paisa, 2 paisae[2] and 1/2 paisa. The word *fulus*, meaning 'copper coin' in Arabic, appears on many of the copper coins. This term was adopted during Ranjit Singh's reign as an additional name for the paisa.

Between the years 1830 and 1840, a silver rupee in Lahore or Amritsar could buy 37.5kg of wheat, 18kg of unrefined cane sugar, 7.7kg of rice or 3.7kg of cotton. Two rupees could buy a sheep, 40–50 rupees a cow and a milking buffalo could be purchased with 100 rupees.[3]

The number of coins in circulation grew as trade developed in the Punjab and northern India under Ranjit Singh's rule (**Map 4**). One of the reasons for this economic prosperity was the silver and gold received from traders for imports and exports moving through the empire. Many Sikhs participated in trade and commerce as it had been encouraged by the fifth Sikh Guru, Guru Arjan.

The location of the Punjab also strengthened its flourishing trade activity. It was one of the great crossroads of southern Asia connecting Central Asia, Afghanistan, India, Tibet and China. The five rivers of the Punjab were an advantage for the efficient transportation of goods although the majority of trade took place on land with goods being carried by camel.

Goods produced and manufactured in, and exported from, the Punjab included grain, sugar, rice, cotton, jewellery, leather, saffron and arms from Lahore. Commodities imported from the rest of British India included spices, copper, woollen fabrics, velvet, silk, satin and muslins. From Afghanistan, the Punjab imported horses, green vegetables and dried fruits, precious stones and opium. Gold was imported from Persia in the form of Venetian ducats along with copper in square flat pieces, needles and nankeen cloth. Gold and silver necklaces were imported from Bokhara. Silver ingots were imported from Tibet and the Chinese frontier along with wool and silk.[4]

In 1832 there were two main trading networks in the Punjab. The Marwani caravans were based in Shehawati and Calcutta, and the Lohani caravans, mostly plying between north-west India and Central Asia were based at Shikarpur (Sindh).

Gold and silver circulated in north-west India in the 1830s via these trading networks. In return for the opium sent to China, Bombay principally received silver trade dollars. Furthermore, 30 or 40 lakh (100,000) rupees in bullion were received annually from Persia in return for goods sent there for trade. Of this bullion, 1 million rupees-worth of silver was sent every year from Bombay to Gwalior, Jaipur, Patiala, Amritsar, and other principal cities in India, where the greater part was coined at the official minting centres and the rest was sold in the bazaars.[5]

The silver, mostly in trade dollars, was sent via Bawnagar and Pali; none of it came from Calcutta. Gold ingots to the value of a few lakh rupees were imported annually by the same road but they seldom found their way further north-west than Jaipur. Camels were the principal method of transport with each animal carrying 4,000 dollars. The silver was said to reach Amritsar from Bombay in 40 days.[2]

Notes
1. Lane-Poole, 1892, 126–28.
2. Plural of Paisa.
3. Singh and Rai, 2008, 237–47.
4. Burnes, 1833, 306–66.
5. Ibid.
6. Lafont, 2002, 92.

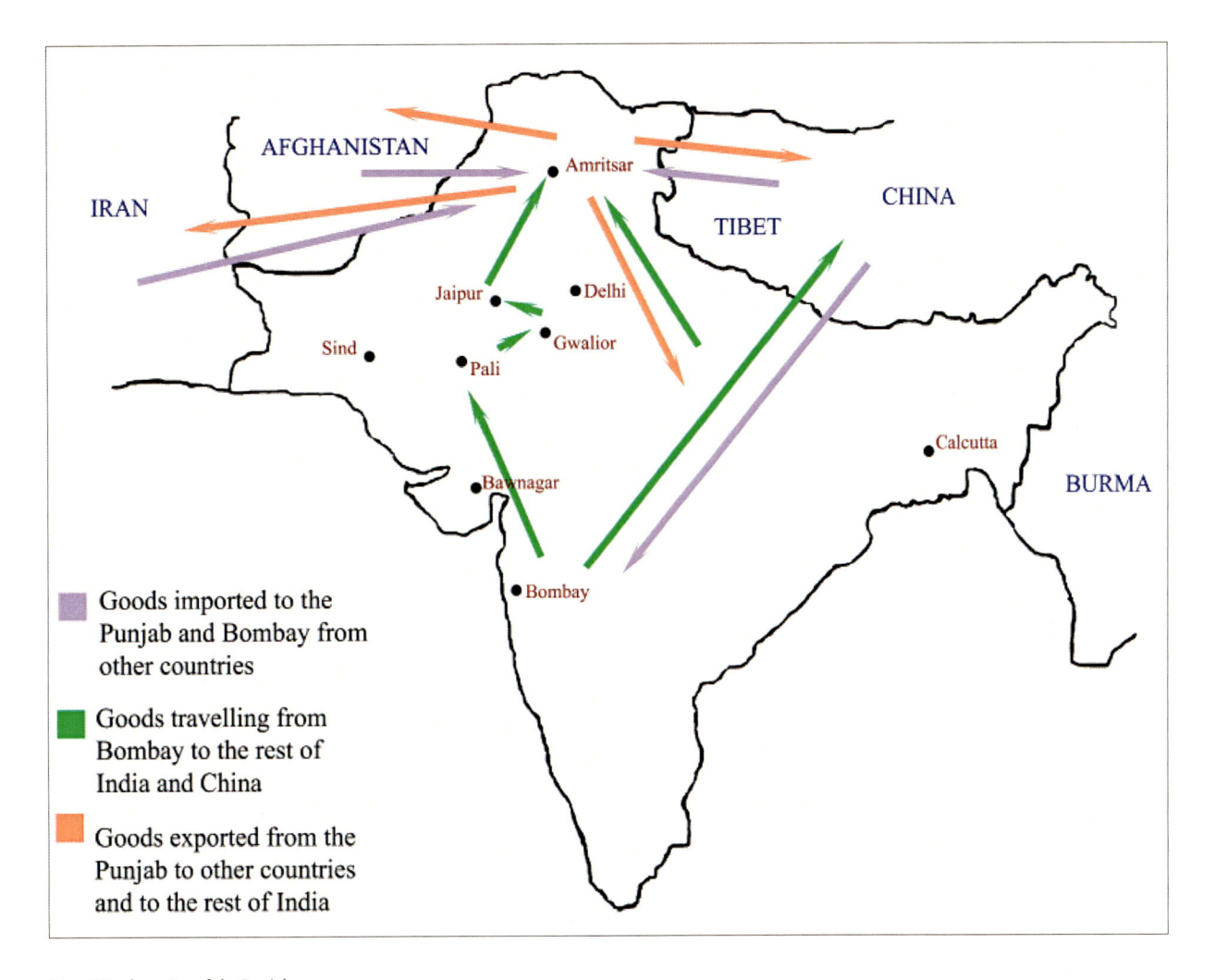

Map 4 Trade routes of the Punjab

Chapter 4
Coin inscriptions

The language used on most Sikh coins was Persian, which had been established by the Mughal government and its official language and therefore it was introduced for coinage in the Punjab as elsewhere.

The Sikh Misals continued the Mughal practice of using Persian inscriptions on their coins. Sikh mohurs and rupees, i.e. the gold and silver coins, bore Persian inscriptions while the Sikh copper coins were often inscribed with the Gurmukhi script. The Gurmukhi legends appeared on paisas issued in Amritsar and in many provincial towns.

As with Iranian and Afghan coins of the 18th and 19th centuries, the legends on Sikh coins appear in verse. This is known in Persian as *beet*, meaning couplet or distich.[1]

The verse often begins at the bottom of the flan and is to be read upwards. The words are not consecutive as they occur in the legend but instead are placed in an elaborate order.

A unique feature that distinguishes Sikh coins from other coins of the Indian subcontinent during the 18th and 19th centuries is the lack of a reference to the name of the current ruler on the coins. Instead, the coins were inscribed with the names of the 1st and 10th Sikh Gurus and were issued in the name of *Akal* (immortal Lord). The Sikh Misal chiefs and Maharaja Ranjit Singh took pride in believing that their triumph over the opposition was not due to any one leader but the result of the Divine One's blessing. For this reason, their coins were struck with the names of Guru Nanak and Guru Gobind Singh, the founders of the Sikh faith and the Khalsa brotherhood. This feature was first noticed by C.J. Rodgers, who wrote: 'Ranjit Singh put his name on nothing, gave his name to nothing. The fort he built at Amritsar is called Gobind Garh;[2] the garden he made there, Ram Bagh.'[3]

The main obverse inscriptions or couplets that feature on Sikh mohurs or rupees are known as the Nanakshahi and Gobindshahi couplets.[4]

C.J. Rodgers suggests that the 'Gobindshahi' inscription has been given this title because the name of the tenth Guru features prominently in the inscription.[5]

In contrast, Surinder Singh notes that the names of both Guru Nanak and Guru Gobind Singh appear on both of the different legends and on every Sikh coin.[6] He writes that it is difficult to distinguish which coins bear the Nanakshahi inscription and which bear the Gobindshahi inscription and, therefore, all Sikh coinage should be referred to as 'Nanakshahi'.[7] Gurprit Singh provides a third possibility. He states that it is difficult to determine precisely how these inscriptions got their titles and, instead, emphasises their convenience: 'it goes without saying that these two couplets have been very helpful and successful in broadly categorising the Sikh coins into two categories.'[8]

Hans Herrli rejects any symbolic meaning for these classes and instead confirms that they are simply technical terms distinguishing two well defined groups of Sikh rupees and mohurs and that they never had an ideological background.[9]

Thus the two differentiating terms – Nanakshahi and Gobindshahi – continue to be used in Sikh numismatics and, because they are useful for distinguishing the legends on the coins, will also be used in this catalogue.

Gobindshahi
During the Khalsa Republic era, Banda Singh Bahadar created an official state legend which was used in official seals that were stamped on the *hukamnamas*, 'official orders', that he issued in 1710.[10] This legend continued to be used by the Sikhs a century later as the inscription on the regularly issued coins.

According to Surinder Singh,[11] the seal impression of Banda Singh, translates from the Persian as:

دیگ تیغ فتح نصرت بیدرنگ
یافت از نانک گوروگوبند سنگ

Degh Tegh Fateh Nusrat Bedrang,
Yaft az Nanak Guru Gobind Singh.[12]

The kettle to feed, the sword to defend, and the resultant victory have been achieved with the spontaneous help received from Guru Nanak to Guru Gobind Singh.

The Gobindshahi inscription occurs on the Sikh coins in the following structure:

دیگ تیغ و فتح نصرت بیدرنگ
یافت از نانک گورگوبند سنگ

Degh Tegh o Fateh Nusrat Bedrang,
Yaft az Nanak Guru Gobind Singh

The kettle to feed, the sword to defend, and the resultant victory have been achieved with the spontaneous help received from Guru Nanak to Guru Gobind Singh.[13]

Five variations of this couplet occur on the coins. They do not, however, alter the basic meaning of the legend; they only differ in minor ways. For example:

دیگ و تیغ و فتح و نصرت بیدرنگ
یافت از نانک گورو گوبند سنگ

Deg o tegh o fath o nusrat bedrang
Yaft az Nanak Guru Gobind Singh

There are several interpretations as to the correct meaning of this legend. The significance of the phrase is the emphasis placed on the receiving or obtaining of Guru Gobind Singh from Guru Nanak. According to the Sikh philosophy the 10 Gurus were the reincarnation of Guru Nanak and, therefore, the part of the legend which reads 'Nanak Guru Gobind Singh' covers the entire period of Guruship, the 1st Guru to the 10th.

This fits in with the idea of the 10 Gurus having one identity along with the absolute supremacy of God.

The notion of *Degh Tegh Fateh* is a development of the 'Miri Piri' (temporal and spiritual) concept initiated by Guru Hargobind, the sixth Sikh Guru, whereby the spiritual powers of the Guru were exercised from the Harmandir and the temporal powers were exercised from the *Akal Takht*.

Nanakshahi

The Nanakshai inscription type that occurs predominantly on coins of the Lahore mint is as follows:

سکه زد بر سیم وزر
فضل سچا صاحب است
فتح گوبند سنگه شاهن
تیغ نانک واهب است

Sikka Zad bar sim va zar fazl sacha sahib ast, fateh Gobind Singh-I-shahan, Tegh Nanak wahib ast

Coin struck in silver and gold by the grace of the true Lord. Of the victory of Gobind, Lion of Kings, Nanak's sword is the provider.[14]

The style of the couplet and the terminology used in the first line strongly resembles the structure and words used in the inscriptions on the coins of Ahmad Shah and Shuja al-Mulk Durrani. According to Herrli[15] the Nanakshahi couplet was originally inspired by a Durrani coin inscription. The similarity can be seen in the three coin inscriptions below:

Inscription on coin of Shuja al-Mulk Durrani (1803–09/1839–42):

سکه زد بر سیم و زور چون مهر و ماه
شاه دین پرور شجاع الملک شاه

*Sikka zad bar sim va zor chun mohar va mah
Shah din pirur Shuja al-Mulk Shah*

The religious king, Shuja al-Mulk Shah, struck coins in silver and gold like the sun and the moon.[16]

Inscription of Ahmad Shah Durrani (1747-1772):

سکه بر زر بزد بفضل اله
شاه عالم پناه احمد شاه

*Sikka bar zar bazd bafsal Illah
Shah Alam p'anna Ahmad Shah*

The world-protecting king Ahmad Shah struck coins in gold by God's grace.[17]

Inscription on coin of Nadir Shah Afsharid (1736-1747):

هشت سلطان بر سلاطین جهان
شاه شاهن نادر صاحبقران

*Hasht Sultan bar Salteen jahan
Shah shahan Nadir Sahibkaran*

Over Sultans of earth is Sultan, Nadir, Shah of Shahs, Sahibkaran.[18]

After examining the above legends it is evident that the Sikhs were influenced by the coins of these contemporary powers.

There are four variations of the Nanakshahi inscription which differ only very slightly. The other common version of the Nanakshai couplet that appears mostly on the coins of Amritsar is formed as thus:

سکا زد بر هر دو عالم فضل سچا صاحب است
فتح گورگوبند سنگ شاهن تیغ نانک وهب است

*Sikka zad bar har do alam fazl sacha sahib ast
Fateh Gur Gobind Singh Shah-I-shahan, Tegh Nanak wahib ast.*

Coin struck in the two worlds (spiritual and secular) by the grace of the True Lord. Nanak is the provider of the sword (power) by which Guru Gobind Singh is victorious.[19]

The two worlds mentioned in this inscription refer to the spiritual and temporal worlds, a term often used in Islamic coin inscriptions. The victory of the tenth Guru along with the provision of Guru Nanak is representative of the Sikh ethos in which all actions, whether successes or defeats, are the will and command of the Guru.

On the second line of the couplet the old Persian title Shah-I Shahan is used. This title meaning 'King of Kings' was common in the Persian tradition and was solely used for the emperors of Iran as can be seen on the inscription of Nadir Shah (above).

The tenth Guru, Gobind Singh, was given this honorary title and praised as the King of the world.

Reverse inscriptions

The reverse inscriptions on Sikh coins vary enormously but usually consist of the mint name, the date and a phrase referring to the reign of the almighty (God).

Again these legends are based on reverse legends of Afghan Durrani coins and are manipulated to comply with the Sikh ideology.

Reverse legend on Sikh coin of Amritsar:

سری امرتسر ضرب
سمبت مانوس میمنت جلوس

*Sri Amritsar Zarb (vs year),
Sambat Manus Maimanat Julus*

Struck in the illustrious Amritsar, in the year of the prosperous human reign.

Reverse legend on coin of Ahmad Shah Durrani coin:

جلوس میمنت مانوس سنه
ضرب پشاور

*Julus Maimanat Manus Sanah 2,
Zarb Peshawar*

Struck in Peshawar in year two of the prosperous human reign.[20]

There are minor structural differences between the reverse legends of the Sikh and Durrani coins. One such difference is the date, for example based on either the Vikrama or Hijri calendars and, another is the phrasing of words. By imitating and manipulating the coin inscriptions of their rival Durrani forces, the Sikhs exerted their authority over the Afghans by giving their inscriptions a Sikh meaning.

The reverse inscriptions vary for each mint and will be translated as and when they occur in the catalogue.

The obverse on the copper coins in the Persian language usually bear short invocations of Guru Nanak or Guru Gobind Singh and display the denomination, mint name and date on the reverse. On occasion the coins have either the Nanakshahi or Gobindshahi couplet.

Gurmukhi inscriptions

Many of the copper coins were inscribed in Gurmukhi, the script of the *Guru Granth Sahib* and the local language of the Sikhs.[21] The use of Gurmukhi was restricted to the copper coins as they were struck by local mints and circulated locally. In comparison gold and silver coins were issued by the state authorities which still required the use of Persian as the official language. Gold and silver coins also travelled outside of the Punjab where it was important for them to be inscribed in Persian, to resemble the Durrani and Mughal coinage they were circulated with. It is also possible that Gurmukhi was more commonly read and understood among the masses and therefore used on copper coins which had lower values and would be more widely circulated in these circles.

The Gurmukhi inscription mostly occurs on the copper coins of Amritsar. The legend focuses on God, the Immortal Lord and Guru Nanak the founder of the Sikh faith:

Obverse inscription:

ਅਕਾਲ ਸਹਾਇ ਗੁਰੂ ਨਾਨਕ ਜੀ

Akal Sahai Guru Nanak Ji

The immortal Lord (God) helps the illustrious Guru Nanak.[22]

Reverse inscription:

ਜਰਬ ਸਰੀ ਅ਼ਬ ਰਤਸਰ ਜੀ
੧੮੮੫

Zarb Sri Amritsar Ji (1885 vs)

Struck at the illustrious Amritsar.[23]

There are also examples of Sikh copper coins inscribed in both the Persian and Gurmukhi scripts with the denomination in Persian. For example:

یک فلوس

Yek Fulus

One fulus (a copper coin denomination)

Reverse inscription (the usual Gurmukhi inscription):

ਅਕਾਲ ਸਹਾਇ ਗੁਰੂ ਨਾਨਕ ਜੀ

Akal Sahai Guru Nanak Ji

The immortal Lord (God) helps the illustrious Guru Nanak.

The use of both Gurmukhi and Persian on a coin suggests that Maharaja Ranjit Singh promoted equality among his subjects. Both the masses and those with a higher status could identify with the message on the coins through their understanding of Persian, Gurmukhi or both languages.

Names for God or the Almighty were also inscribed in the Nagri script on some of the coins, in addition to the standard Nanakshahi inscription. It is possible that the words *Om* or *Ram* were included to appeal to the Hindu population of the Punjab. The variety of languages and scripts used on the Sikh coins illustrate the Maharaja's principles of equality, tolerance and respect, values that were initiated by Guru Nanak. It is also possible that Ranjit Singh required respect, support and admiration from his subjects and by using the various languages he appealed to the different community groups prevalent in the Punjab.

To view a chart detailing some of the similarities and differences between Gurmukhi and Persian numerals, see Appendix 3.

Notes

1. Haim, 2008, 801.
2. Gobind Garh, 'House of Gobind'. Gobind was the 10th Sikh Guru.
3. Rodgers, 1881, 83.
4. The term 'Shahi' meaning 'of the government of'.
5. Rodgers, 1881, 78.
6. Singh, S. 2004, 67.
7. Ibid.
8. Singh, G. 2002–03, 102.
9. Herrli, 2004, 32.
11. Ibid.
12. It is important to note that the Persian inscriptions are transliterated according to the Sikh and Punjabi pronunciations of the words and phrases.
13. Ibid.
14. Herrli, 2004, 30.
15. Herrli, 2004, 30.
16. Codrington, 1904, 103.
17. Ibid, 102
18. Ibid, 99
19. Lafont, 2002, 93.
20. Rodgers, 1885, 69.
21. Gurmukhi was introduced by Guru Angad Dev Ji, the second Sikh Guru.
22. Herrli, 2004, 89.
23. Ibid.

Chapter 5
Dates and Symbols on Sikh Coins

The Vikrama Samvat calendar
Most Sikh coins feature a prominent date in Persian numerals on the reverse. This date is known as the Vikrama Samvat date. The Vikrama Samvat years are based on a lunar calendar used mostly by Sikhs and Hindus in north India, western India and Nepal. Indian tradition claims that the calendar was established by the Indian Emperor Vikramaditya of Ujjain (102 BC–AD 15) after his victory over the Sakas in 56 BC.

The years of the Vikrama Sambat era are converted to the Gregorian calendar by subtracting 57 years: vs year − 57 = AD year. To view a vs/AD conversion chart, see Appendix 4.

The dates of the Sikh general assemblies that met twice a year at Amritsar were determined by the Vikrama Samvat calendar of religious festivals. The spring 'Sarbat Khalsa' fell on the first day of the month of Visakh (April) and the winter assembly fell in the middle of the month of Kartikka (November), the month of Diwali.

The display of the vs date on Sikh coins started from the initial Sikh Misal coinage and continued up until the end of the Sikh Empire in 1849.

The gold mohurs and silver rupees of Amritsar and Lahore were issued with a vs year of 1884 (AD 1827), 1885 (AD 1828) or 1888 (AD 1831) on the reverse. It is uncertain why these particular years appear on these coins, particularly as the coins were continuously minted between AD 1775 and AD 1849. One theory argues that it is related to a tax issue. An Indian tax on capital, known as *Bhatta*, involved the devaluation of coins every year. In an attempt to discourage this practice in states that had abolished this tax, a 'frozen' year was put on the coins.[1] However, on the obverse of these coins the last two numbers of the actual date are inscribed in tiny figures. This contradicts the above theory as the coins could still be devalued and still display the correct date of issue.

Herrli suggests, more plausibly, that the appearance of the 'frozen' years on the coins of Lahore and Amritsar is an outwardly visible mark symbolising the reform of a currency or reorganisation of the mint.[2]

Symbols
The coins of the Sikh Misal period are simple in design compared with those issued by Ranjit Singh. The addition of ornate and royal symbols such as, umbrellas and flags, on the coins issued under the reign of the Maharaja, suggest the Sikh Empire's economic prosperity.

The elaborate calligraphic Persian inscription is regarded as the main design feature of the Sikh coins, however, the various symbols and marks contribute to the overall elegant style.

Punch dagger
The Sikh Misal silver rupees issued in the years vs 1841 and vs 1842 have the symbol of a *kartar*, 'punch dagger' on the reverse.

Masood ul Hasan Khokhar[3] writes that the *kartar* is one of the five Sikh symbols that a practicing Sikh must wear and that is why it features on the coins. This is unlikely because the actual Sikh symbol belonging to the five Ks is the '*Kirpan*' or sword;[4] hence many Sikhs wear a small sword as part of their code of conduct (*rahit*).[5]

Weapons such as the sword and the punch dagger were respected by the *Khalsa* as weapons that could be used to protect the faith against injustice and tyranny. It is probable that the Sikh Misals had the punch dagger image on their coins as a symbol of their victory and as a sign of protection against the foreign invasions for the local people.

Following close examination of the 11 Sikh Misal punch dagger coins in the British Museum collection it would appear that only the coins adopting the 'Gobindshahi' couplet have the punch dagger symbol on the reverse. This could relate to the 'Gobindshahi' couplet stating victory *Degh Tegh Fateh* 'Victory to the sword and the kettle' and the punch dagger being a victorious symbol, however, there is limited evidence to support this relationship.

Leaf
The leaf motif appeared on the reverse side of some of the Sikh coins towards the end of the 18th century. After 1801 the leaf was placed on every Sikh coin until the end of Sikh rule in 1849. The distinctive leaf makes Sikh coins instantly distinguishable from contemporary coins from India and Afghanistan.

Several interpretations of the meaning of this symbol exist but there is limited evidence to support any single theory. Valentine refers to the leaf as a 'pipal' leaf (*ficus religiosa*), suggesting that it is a favourite sign or mark of the Sikhs.[6] The pipal tree is the sacred fig tree native to the Punjab, Nepal, Bangladesh and Sri Lanka. It is considered holy in the Hindu and Buddhist traditions. The leaves of the tree are heart shaped with a distinctive extended tip.

R.T. Somaiya argues that the Ber leaf is depicted on the coins rather than a pipal leaf. The Ber tree (*zizyphus jujbe*) is present in the precincts of the golden temple complex in Amritsar. Often referred to as 'Dukhbanjani', sorrow remover in Punjabi, the tree is revered by Sikhs for its miraculous powers. Tradition records that the fourth Sikh Guru, Guru Ram Das sat under the tree whilst supervising the construction of the sacred pool. As S.J.S. Pall writes, 'It is sufficient to say that Ber is an important tree and berries in Amritsar had miraculous powers, hence the selection of Ber on Sikh coins.'[7]

Surinder Singh links the leaf motif to the *Chalisa* famine that occurred in northern India in 1783–84.[8] He suggests that the Sikhs placed a leaf on their coins to seek the blessings of their Gurus, to symbolize fertility and prosperity and to give thanks for their wellbeing.[9]

Herrli does not believe that the Sikh die-cutters aimed to show the leaf of a particular, botanically identifiable plant, but rather that they intended to illustrate the general idea of a leaf.[10] The various styles of the leaf depicted on the coins of different mints in the British Museum collection support Herrli's opinion.

Peacock tail

Another symbol which features prominently on many of the coins minted in Amritsar during Ranjit Singh's reign is the peacock tail or double branch. Coins with this symbol are often called the 'Moran Shahi' coin. It is believed that a dancing girl from Kashmir called 'Moran' was adored by the Maharaja and she convinced Ranjit Singh to strike coins with her name. The Maharaja allegedly put a symbol of a peacock's tail[11] on the coins of Amritsar, representing his love and affection for the girl.

The Sikh religious leaders of the Akal Takht[12] questioned the Maharaja on his affair with the Muslim dancing girl to which Ranjit Singh pleaded guilty and was fined for his actions.[13]

Sikh numismatists and historians have debated whether the symbol on the coins is that of a peacock's tail or whether it is simply a variation of the leaf symbol.

C.J. Rodgers claims that the double branch is indeed a peacock's tail and therefore is the sign of Moran.[14] Lance Dane challenges this opinion by reviewing Ranjit Singh's devotion to the Sikh Gurus:

> To Ranjit Singh the Guru was the Sacha Padshah, the true King, with himself as his humble servant. Out of his out-flowing devotion he ordered the coins of his Empire to be struck in the name of the Guru.[15]

R.T. Somaiya comments on the misrepresented symbol as a bunch of Ber tree fruits. With the humiliation of the affair, Ranjit Singh sent Moran away after he was charged over the incident. For this reason, Somaiya feels that it would have been impossible for Ranjit Singh to have publicised these events by striking coins in the name of Moran.[16]

An alternative theory to those mentioned above is provided by Raijasbir Singh. He suggests that the double branch is the mark of the earlier Bhangi Misal. Ranjit Singh's rule replaced that of the Bhangi Misal and, for this reason, he adopted this symbol for the Amritsar coins as a mark of his prosperity and victory. Raijasbir Singh believes that the Moran Shahi coin story was invented to undermine the personality of the Maharaja.[17]

A close examination of this symbol on the four coins of this type in the British Museum collection reveals a small stem, which suggests that the symbol is that of a plant, a double branch or a variation of the leaf motif, as opposed to a peacock tail.

Small round decorative symbol

A small round decorative symbol on three of the coins of the Amritsar mint in the British Museum collection has also been connected to the dancing girl Moran. It is claimed that the symbol represents a thumb mirror known as the 'arsi', which would have been worn by dancing girls at the time. These coins are known as the 'Arsiwala Shahi' coins. There is no evidence to suggest that this symbol represented Moran. Instead, it seems more likely that it is simply a decorative ornament or rosette contributing to the elaborate design of the coin.

Canopies, tridents and flags

Further symbols including canopies, tridents and flags appear on the coins issued under Ranjit Singh.

In the Sikh practice it is customary to keep a canopy above the *Guru Granth Sahib*. This reinforces the 'living Guru' ideal as the ten previous Sikh Gurus often sat under a canopy as did kings and princes. Similarly, in the Hindu tradition, placing a canopy in a temple above the deities is a common practice. The canopy symbol on the coins is suggestive of the prime role of the Guru within the Sikh faith or it may represent the royalty of the Maharaja.

The trident also features on some of the coins from the Amritsar mint. This representation of the Hindu deity, Lord Shiva, may have been used to display tolerance and unify the different faiths of the Punjab.

The flag traditionally used to represent a nation or kingdom appears on many of the coins, it is possible that in this instance the flag is a battle standard symbolising power and strength.

Mughal and Afghan influences

The coins issued by the Mughals and the Durranis had the most influence on the design and content of the Sikh coins.

The Mughal emperor Aurangzeb replaced marginal inscriptions on coins with the ruler's simple titles or an appropriate couplet on the obverse and the following Persian formula on the reverse:

سمبت جلوس میمنت مانوس

Sambat julus maimanut manus

The year of the prosperous human reign.

This formula was also adopted by the Afghan Durrani dynasty (see Chapter 4).

The Sikh coins followed the pattern of using a religious couplet on the obverse and in many cases using this reverse formula with the addition of a mint name and the date of issue.

By using the Persian language, a language that their contemporary rulers understood, the Sikh leaders were able to glorify their Gurus, while making their coins distinct at the same time. The Sikhs manipulated existing coin legends and designs to create an identity for their own coins.[18]

Many of the symbols used on Sikh coins were also originally used by Mughal rulers on their coins. The coins of Shah Alam II (1759–88) have symbols of fish, the trident (*trisul*) and the state umbrella. It is not known what the actual meaning of these symbols is and it is unlikely that they are distinguishing state marks because many states adopt them. As Codrington commented on the symbols on Mughal coins:

> 'It has been the endeavour of several Indian numismatists to reduce them to order and locate their use; but it is a very difficult matter, for many of them have been used by several states, and many states have used several symbols at different times, and local knowledge and tradition give but little help.'

It is clear, however, that the Sikhs continued to use these symbols on their coins, perhaps reflecting their belief that their rule was equal to that of the previous Mughal dynasty.

On the coins of Muhammad Akbar II (1806–37), the symbol of the state umbrella falls directly over the word 'sahib', meaning master or lord. Similarly, the canopies on the Sikh coins fall on top of the word Guru. This does not appear to be a coincidental location for the symbol and, instead, may have been a mark of respect. This design was adopted by Maharaja Ranjit Singh (see catalogue nos. 115 and 119).

Civic copper coinage issued in Afghanistan during the 18th and 19th centuries often had decorative images on the obverse of the coins such as birds, peacocks, flowers, leaves and dots. The denomination 'fulus' was inscribed on the reverse of the copper coins.[19] Similarly, the Sikhs modelled many of their copper paisas on the Afghan copper coins. The use of bird, flower and leaf images is common on copper coins minted in Amritsar, Peshawar and Kashmir (see catalogue no. 464).

Notes
1. Goran and Wiggins, 1981, 12.
2. Herrli, 2004, 33.
3. Khokhar, 1987–88, 26.
4. The five Ks are five outwardly symbols beginning with the letter K, worn by baptised Sikhs.
5. Pall, 2001, 201. 'The Code of Conduct, as per the tradition and as mentioned in Rehatnama only prescribes the wearing of a sword as one of the requirements.'
6. Valentine, 1920, 126.
7. Somaiya, 1994, 1.
8. Chalisa literally means 'of the 40th' as it occurred in VS 1840.
9. Singh, S. 2004, 76. A severe drought caused ponds, tanks and wells to dry up and led to many deaths. The territory stretching from Multan to Bengal was affected by the 'Chalisa' famine also involving the Punjab. During the famine the Sikhs contributed substantially by helping to feed the poor. In March 1784 the rains began and slowly the conditions improved.
10. Herrli, 2004, 25.
11. *Moran* meaning peacock in the Punjabi language.
12. Seat of political authority in Amritsar.
13. Having such associations with women of the Islamic faith was forbidden in Sikhism.
14. Rodgers, 1881, 72.
15. Dance, 1981, 132.
16. Somaiya, 1994, 2.
17. Raijasbir, 1995, 124.
18. For further information on coin inscriptions see Chapter 4.
19. Valentine, 1911, 161–83.

Chapter 6
Catalogue

Mint Amritsar

To view referenced mint marks, see Appendix 2.

Gold coins

1

Gold double mohur with flower patterns on the obverse and a leaf on the reverse

AD 1826 /VS 1883
Authority: Ranjit Singh
Inscription: Nanakshahi couplet

Obverse: Persian

سکا زد بر هر دو عالم فضل سچا صاحب است فتح
تیغ گورگوبند سنگ شاہ نانک وھب است

Transliteration
Sikka zad bar har do alam fazl sacha sahib ast Fateh tegh Gur Gobind Singh Shah, Nanak wahib ast.

Translation
The coin struck through each of the two worlds by the grace of the true Lord. Of the victory gained by the sword of Guru Gobind Singh Shah Nanak is the provider

Reverse: Persian

سری امرتسرجیو ضرب جلوس میمنت بخت اکال
تخت سنا

Transliteration
Sri Amritsar jiyo zarb Julus maimanat bakht Akal Takht sanah

Translation
Struck at Illustrious Amritsar under the prosperous rule of the fortunate Akal Takht

21.1g   30mm
1874,1001.1 Guthrie collection

2

Gold double mohur with flower patterns on the obverse and a leaf on the reverse

AD 1827/VS 1884
Authority: Ranjit Singh
Inscription: Nanakshahi couplet (as no. 1)

23.9g   28mm
1912,0709.210 Bleazby collection

3

Gold mohur with a trident on the obverse and a leaf on the reverse

AD 1828/VS 1885
Authority: Ranjit Singh

Obverse: Gurmukhi

ਅਕਾਲ ਸਹਾਈ ਗੁਰੁਨਾਨਕਜੀ

Transliteration
Akaal sahai Gur Nanak Ji.

Translation
The immortal Lord (akaal) helps the illustrious Guru Nanak

Reverse: Gurmukhi

ਜਰਬ ਸੀ ਅਬਿਰਟਸਰਜੀ ੧੮੮੫

Transliteration
Zarb sri Amritsar ji 1885.

Translation
Struck at the illustrious Amritsar 1885

9.7g   21mm
1884,0502.1 C.J. Rodgers collection

4

Gold half mohur with flower patterns on the obverse and a leaf on the reverse

AD 1801/VS 1858
Authority: Ranjit Singh
Inscription: Nanakshahi couplet (as no. 1)

10.7g   21mm
1850,1121.4 Cureton collection

5

Gold half mohur with a fish on the obverse and a leaf on the reverse

AD 1804/VS 1861
Authority: Ranjit Singh
Inscription: Nanakshahi couplet (as no. 1)

10.7g   20mm
1912,0709.208 Bleazby collection

6

Gold half mohur with dots on the obverse, mirror symbol and a leaf on the reverse

AD 1806/VS 1863
Authority: Ranjit Singh
Arsiwalashahi coin
Inscription: Nanakshahi couplet (as no. 1)

10.7g   20mm
1912,0709.209 Bleazby collection

7

Gold half mohur with small mint mark on the obverse and a leaf on the reverse

AD 1811/VS 1868
Authority: Ranjit Singh
Inscription: Nanakshahi couplet (as no. 1)

10.7g   20mm
1920,0514.31 Doyle Smithe collection

Catalogue Nos 8–18

8

Gold half mohur with dot patterns on the obverse and a leaf on the reverse

AD 1806/VS 1863
Authority: Ranjit Singh
Inscription: Nanakshahi couplet (as no. 1)

10.6g   20mm
1850,0808.30 Amherst collection

Silver coins

9

Silver rupee

AD 1778/VS 1835
Authority: Sikh Misal
Inscription: Nanakshahi couplet (as no. 1)

11.3g   20mm
1936,1017.17 Baldwin collection

10

Silver rupee

AD 1777/VS 1834
Authority: Sikh Misal
Inscription: Nanakshahi couplet (as no. 1)

11.2g   20mm
1936,1017.55 Baldwin collection

11

Silver rupee

AD 1779/VS 1836
Authority: Sikh Misal
Inscription: Nanakshahi couplet (as no. 1)

11.0g   20mm
1936,1017.18 Baldwin collection

12

Silver rupee

AD 1779/VS 1836
Authority: Sikh Misal
Inscription: Nanakshahi couplet (as no. 1)

11.1g   21mm
1912,0709.304 Bleazby collection

13

Silver rupee

AD 1780/VS 1837
Authority: Sikh Misal
Inscription: Nanakshahi couplet (as no. 1)

11.1g   20mm
1912,0709.305 Bleazby collection

14

Silver rupee

AD 1781/VS 1838
Authority: Sikh Misal
Inscription: Nanakshahi couplet (as no. 1)

10.8g   20mm
1912,0709.306 Bleazby collection

15

Silver rupee with a small punch dagger on the reverse

AD 1784/VS 1841
Authority: Sikh Misal
Inscription: Gobindshahi couplet

Obverse: Persian

دیگ تیغ و فتح نصرت بیدرنگ یافت از نانک گورگوبند سنگ

Transliteration
Deg tegh o fath nusrat bedrang Yaft az Nanak Gur Gobind Singh

Translation
Abundance, power and victory [and] assistance without delay are the gift of Nanak [and] Guru Gobind Singh

Reverse: Persian

سری امرتسر ضرب سمبت مانوس میمنت جلوس

Transliteration
Sri Amritsar zarb Sambat manus maimanat julus.

Translation
Struck at the illustrious Amritsar in the samvat year of the prosperous human reign

11.0g   20mm
1912,0709.307 Bleazby collection

16

Silver rupee with a small leaf on the obverse and a small punch dagger on the reverse

AD 1784/VS 1841
Authority: Sikh Misal
Inscription: Gobindshahi couplet (as no. 15)

10.8g   20mm
1903,1009.1 Talbot collection

17

Silver rupee with a small leaf on the obverse and a small punch dagger on the reverse

AD 1784/VS 1841
Authority: Sikh Misal
Inscription: Gobindshahi couplet (as no. 15)

11.0g   20mm
1907,0702.24 Government of the Central Provinces of India

18

Silver rupee with a small leaf on the obverse and a small punch dagger on the reverse

AD 1784/VS 1841
Authority: Sikh Misal
Inscription: Gobindshahi couplet (as no. 15)

11.0g   20mm
1907,0702.21 Government of the Central Provinces of India

Catalogue Nos 19–29

19
Silver rupee with a small leaf on the obverse and a small punch dagger on the reverse

AD 1784/VS 1841
Authority: Sikh Misal
Inscription: Gobindshahi couplet (as no. 15)

10.9g   20mm
1907,0702.19 Government of the Central Provinces of India

20
Silver rupee with a small leaf on the obverse and a small punch dagger on the reverse

AD 1784/VS 1841
Authority: Sikh Misal
Inscription: Gobindshahi couplet (as no. 15)

10.8g   20mm
1907,0702.20 Government of the Central Provinces of India

21
Silver rupee with small dots on the obverse

AD 1784/VS 1841
Authority: Sikh Misal
Inscription: Nanakshahi couplet

Obverse: Persian

سکا زد بر هر دو عالم فضل سچا صاحب است فتح
تیغ گوروگوبند سنگ شاه نانک وهب است

Transliteration
Sikka zad bar har do alam fazl sacha sahib ast
Fateh tegh Guru Gobind Singh Shah, Nanak wahib ast

Translation
The coin struck through each of the two worlds by the grace of the true lord. Of the victory of Gobind Singh, king of kings, Nanak's sword is the provider

Reverse: Persian

سری امرتسر جیو ضرب جلوس میمنت بخت اکال تخت سنہ

Transliteration
Sri Amritsar jiyo zarb julus maimanat bakht akal takht sanah.

Translation
Struck at illustrious Amritsar under the prosperous rule of the fortunate Akal Takht

11.3g   20mm
1903,1009.2 Talbot collection

22
Silver rupee with a small flower on the obverse and a punch dagger on the reverse

AD 1785/VS 1842
Authority: Sikh Misal
Inscription: Gobindshahi couplet (as no. 15)

10.8g   20mm
1865,0803.73 Stubbs collection

23
Silver rupee with a small flower pattern on the obverse and a leaf on the reverse

AD 1788/VS 1845
Authority: Sikh Misal
Inscription: Nanakshahi couplet (as no. 1)

11.0g   20mm
1912,0709.310 Bleazby collection

24
Silver rupee with a small flower on the obverse and a punch dagger on the reverse

AD 1785/VS 1842
Authority: Sikh Misal
Inscription: Gobinshahi couplet (as no. 15)

10.9g   20mm
1912,0709.309 Bleazby collection

25
Silver rupee with small dots on the obverse

AD 1785/VS 1842
Authority: Sikh Misal
Inscription: Nanakshahi couplet (as no. 1)

11.3g   20mm
1887,0508.4 Theobald collection

26
Silver rupee with a leaf on the reverse

AD 1789/VS 1846
Authority: Sikh Misal
Inscription: Nanakshahi couplet (as no. 1)

11.1g   20mm
1936,1017.24 Baldwin collection

27
Silver rupee with dot patterns on the obverse and a leaf in the centre on the reverse

AD 1793/VS 1850
Authority: Sikh Misal
Inscription: Nanakshahi couplet (as no. 1)

11.0g   20mm
1912,0709.313 Bleazby collection

28
Silver rupee with dot patterns on the obverse and a leaf in the centre on the reverse

AD 1796/VS 1853
Authority: Sikh Misal
Inscription: Nanakshahi couplet (as no. 1)

11.0g   20mm
1887,0508.2 Theobald collection

29
Silver rupee with small flower on the obverse and a punch dagger on the reverse

AD 1797/VS 1854
Authority: Sikh Misal
Inscription: Gobindshahi couplet (as no. 15)

10.7g   22mm
1912,0709.311 Bleazby collection

30
Silver rupee with small dots on the obverse and leaf in centre on the reverse

AD 1798/VS 1855
Authority: Sikh Misal
Inscription: Nanakshahi couplet (as no. 1)

10.9g 22mm
1912,0709.312 Bleazby collection

31
Silver rupee with small dots on the obverse and a leaf on the reverse

AD 1799/VS 1856
Authority: Sikh Misal
Inscription: Nanakshahi couplet (as no. 1)

11.1g 21mm
1912,0709.314 Bleazby collection

32
Silver rupee with small flowers and leaf on the reverse

AD 1799/VS 1856
Authority: Sikh Misal
Inscription: Nanakshahi couplet (as no. 1)

10.8g 21mm
OR 5036

33
Silver rupee with small dots on the obverse and a leaf on the reverse

AD 1801/VS 1858
Authority: Ranjit Singh
Inscription: Nanakshahi couplet (as no. 1)

10.8g 21mm
1920,0722.75 Houston collection

34
Silver rupee with a small punch dagger on the obverse and leaf on the reverse

AD 1802/VS 1859
Authority: Ranjit Singh
Inscription: Gobindshahi couplet (as no. 15)

10.8g 21mm
1912,0709.248 Bleazby collection

35
Silver rupee with a small punch dagger on the obverse and leaf on the reverse

AD 1802/VS 1859
Authority: Ranjit Singh
Inscription: Gobindshahi couplet (as no. 15)

10.6g 21mm
1922,0424.2372 Whitehead collection

36
Silver rupee with a double sprig with buds on the reverse

AD 1804/VS 1861
Authority: Ranjit Singh
Morashahi coin
Inscription: Nanakshahi couplet (as no. 1)

11.2g 22mm
1912,0709.250 Bleazby collection

37
Silver rupee with a fish on the obverse and a leaf on the reverse

AD 1804/VS 1861
Authority: Ranjit Singh
Inscription: Nanakshahi couplet (as no. 1)

10.9g 21mm
1903,1009.3 Talbot collection

38
Silver rupee with a fish on the obverse and a double sprig with buds on the reverse

AD 1805/VS 1862
Authority: Ranjit Singh
Morashahi coin
Inscription: Nanakshahi couplet (as no. 1)

11.1g 22mm
1853,0301.1089 Eden collection

39
Silver rupee with a fish on the obverse and a double sprig with buds on the reverse

AD 1805/VS 1862
Authority: Ranjit Singh
Morashahi coin
Inscription: Nanakshahi couplet (as no. 1)

11.1g 21mm
1853,0301.1087 Eden collection

40
Silver rupee with a double sprig with buds on the reverse

AD 1805/VS 1862
Authority: Ranjit Singh
Morashahi coin
Inscription: Nanakshahi couplet (as no. 1)

11.2g 21mm
1912,0709.252 Bleazby collection

41
Silver rupee with a mirror symbol on the reverse

AD 1806/VS 1863
Authority: Ranjit Singh
Arsiwalashahi coin
Inscription: Nanakshahi couplet (as no. 1)

Catalogue Nos 42–53

11.1g 22mm
1853,0301.1090 Eden collection

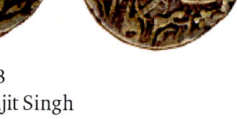

42
Silver rupee with dots and a mint mark on the obverse and a leaf on the reverse

AD 1805/VS 1862
Authority: Ranjit Singh
Inscription: Nanakshahi couplet (as no. 1)

11.1g 22mm
OR 1719

43
Silver rupee with small dots and a leaf on the reverse

AD 1807/VS 1864
Authority: Ranjit Singh
Inscription: Nanakshahi couplet (as no. 1)

11.0g 22mm
1887,0508.3 Theobald collection

44
Silver rupee with small dots and a leaf on the reverse

AD 1808/VS 1865
Authority: Ranjit Singh
Inscription: Nanakshahi couplet (as no. 1)

10.9g 22mm
1912,0709.254 Bleazby collection

45
Silver rupee with small dots and a leaf on the reverse

AD 1808/VS 1865
Authority: Ranjit Singh
Inscription: Nanakshahi couplet (as no. 1)

11.0g 20mm
1868,1233.16 M.G. Clerk collection

46
Silver rupee with a leaf on the obverse and flower on the reverse

AD 1809/VS 1866
Authority: Ranjit Singh
Inscription: Nanakshahi couplet (as no. 1)

11.1g 20mm
1912,0709.255 Bleazby collection

47
Silver rupee with a dot flower on the obverse and a leaf on the reverse

AD 1810/VS 1867
Authority: Ranjit Singh
Inscription: Nanakshahi couplet (as no. 1)

10.9g 21mm
1912,0709.256 Bleazby collection

48
Silver rupee with a dot flower on the obverse and a leaf on the reverse

AD 1811/VS 1868
Authority: Ranjit Singh
Inscription: Nanakshahi couplet (as no. 1)

10.7g 22mm
1912,0709.258 Bleazby collection

49
Silver rupee with flower on the obverse and a leaf on the reverse

AD 1811/VS 1868
Authority: Ranjit Singh
Inscription: Nanakshahi couplet (as no. 1)

10.8g 21mm
1912,0709.259 Bleazby collection

50
Silver rupee with small dots on the obverse and a leaf on the reverse

AD 1812/VS 1869
Authority: Ranjit Singh
Inscription: Nanakshahi couplet (as no. 1)

11.2g 23mm
1912,0709.260 Bleazby collection

51
Silver rupee with a leaf on the obverse and a flower on the reverse

AD 1812/VS 1869
Authority: Ranjit Singh
Inscription: Nanakshahi couplet (as no. 1)

11.1g 22mm
1912,0709.261 Bleazby collection

52
Silver rupee with a leaf on the obverse and flowers on the reverse

AD 1813/VS 1870
Authority: Ranjit Singh
Inscription: Nanakshahi couplet (as no. 1)

11.1g 21mm
1912,0709.262 Bleazby collection

53
Silver rupee with a leaf on the obverse and flowers on the reverse

AD 1815/VS 1872
Authority: Ranjit Singh
Inscription: Nanakshahi couplet (as no. 1)

11.1g 22mm
1912,0709.263 Bleazby collection

Catalogue Nos 54–65

54
Silver rupee with a mint mark on the obverse and a leaf and dot flowers on the reverse

AD 1816/VS 1873
Authority: Ranjit Singh
Inscription: Nanakshahi couplet (as no. 1)

11.1g   22mm
1912,0709.264 Bleazby collection

55
Silver rupee with a mint mark on the obverse and a leaf and dot flowers on the reverse

AD 1816/VS 1873
Authority: Ranjit Singh
Inscription: Nanakshahi couplet (as no. 1)

11.1g   22mm
1874,1001.2 Guthrie collection

56
Silver rupee with flower patterns on the obverse and a leaf and trident on the reverse

AD 1817/VS 1874
Authority: Ranjit Singh
Inscription: Nanakshahi couplet (as no. 1)

11.0g   21mm
1903,1009.4 Talbot collection

57
Silver rupee with a mint mark on the obverse and a leaf on the reverse

AD 1817/VS 1874
Authority: Ranjit Singh
Inscription: Nanakshahi couplet (as no. 1)

11.1g   22mm
1912,0709.265 Bleazby collection

58
Silver rupee with a mint mark on the obverse and a leaf on the reverse

AD 1818/VS 1875
Authority: Ranjit Singh
Inscription: Nanakshahi couplet (as no. 1)

11.1g   22mm
1887,0508.5 Theobald collection

59
Silver rupee with a mint mark on the obverse and a leaf on the reverse

AD 1819/VS 1876
Authority: Ranjit Singh
Inscription: Nanakshahi couplet (as no. 1)

11.1g   22mm
1853,0606.46 Strachey collection

60
Silver rupee with a mint mark on the obverse and a leaf on the reverse

AD 1819/VS 1876
Authority: Ranjit Singh
Inscription: Nanakshahi couplet (as no. 1)

11.1g   22mm
1912,0709.266 Bleazby collection

61
Silver rupee with a mint mark on the obverse and a leaf on the reverse

AD 1820/VS 1877
Authority: Ranjit Singh
Inscription: Nanakshahi couplet (as no. 1)

11.0g   22mm
1874,1001.5 Guthrie collection

62
Silver rupee with a flower pattern on the obverse and a leaf on the reverse

AD 1821/VS 1878
Authority: Ranjit Singh
Inscription: Nanakshahi couplet (as no. 1)

11.0g   22mm
1912,0709.268 Bleazby collection

63
Silver rupee with a flower pattern on the obverse and a leaf on the reverse

AD 1822/VS 1879
Authority: Ranjit Singh
Inscription: Nanakshahi couplet (as no. 1)

11.1g   23mm
OR 5037

64
Silver rupee with a mint mark on the obverse and a leaf on the reverse

AD 1822/VS 1879
Authority: Ranjit Singh
Inscription: Nanakshahi couplet (as no. 1)

11.0g   22mm
1912,0709.269 Bleazby collection

65
Silver rupee with a mint mark on the obverse and a leaf on the reverse

AD 1823/VS 1880
Authority: Ranjit Singh
Inscription: Nanakshahi couplet (as no. 1)

11.2g   23mm
1887,0508.11 Theobald collection

Catalogue Nos 66–77

66
Silver rupee with a star pattern on the obverse and a leaf on the reverse

AD 1823/VS 1880
Authority: Ranjit Singh
Inscription: Nanakshahi couplet (as no. 1)

11.2g   24mm
1912,0709.270 Bleazby collection

67
Silver rupee with a mint mark on the obverse and a leaf on the reverse

AD 1824/VS 1881
Authority: Ranjit Singh
Inscription: Nanakshahi couplet (as no. 1)

11.0g   23mm
1912,0709.271 Bleazby collection

68
Silver rupee with a mint mark on the obverse and a leaf on the reverse

AD 1825/VS 1882
Authority: Ranjit Singh
Inscription: Nanakshahi couplet (as no. 1)

11.1g   24mm
1887,0508.7 Theobald collection

69
Silver rupee with a mint mark on the obverse and a leaf on the reverse

AD 1826/VS 1883
Authority: Ranjit Singh
Inscription: Nanakshahi couplet (as no. 1)

11.2g   25mm
1912,0709.272 Bleazby collection

70
Silver rupee with a mint mark on the obverse and a leaf on the reverse

AD 1827/VS 1884
Authority: Ranjit Singh
Inscription: Nanakshahi couplet (as no. 1)

11.1g   23mm
1912,0709.273 Bleazby collection

71
Silver rupee with a mint mark on the obverse and a leaf on the reverse

AD 1827/VS 1884
Authority: Ranjit Singh
Inscription: Nanakshahi couplet (as no. 1)

11.1g   22mm
1912,0709.275 Bleazby collection

72
Silver rupee with a mint mark and numerals 87 on the obverse and a leaf on the reverse

AD 1827/VS 1884
Authority: Ranjit Singh
Inscription: Nanakshahi couplet (as no. 1)

11.1g   23mm
1912,0709.276 Bleazby collection

73
Silver rupee with a mint mark and numerals 90 on the obverse and a leaf on the reverse

AD 1827/VS 1884
Authority: Ranjit Singh
Inscription: Nanakshahi couplet (as no. 1)

11.1g   23mm
1912,0709.277 Bleazby collection

74
Silver rupee with a mint mark on the obverse and a leaf on the reverse

AD 1827/VS 1884
Authority: Ranjit Singh
Inscription: Nanakshahi couplet (as no. 1)

11.2g   23mm
OR 5039

75
Silver rupee with a mint mark and numerals 91 on the obverse and a leaf on the reverse

AD 1827/VS 1884
Authority: Ranjit Singh
Inscription: Nanakshahi couplet (as no. 1)

11.0g   23mm
1912,0709.278 Bleazby collection

76
Silver rupee with an umbrella symbol on the obverse and a leaf on the reverse

AD 1828/VS 1885
Authority: Ranjit Singh
Inscription: Nanakshahi couplet (as no. 1)

11.1g   23mm
1912,0709.289 Bleazby collection

77
Silver rupee with a mint mark on the obverse and a leaf on the reverse

AD 1827/VS 1884
Authority: Ranjit Singh
Inscription: Nanakshahi couplet (as no. 1)

11.1g   23mm
1912,0709.279 Bleazby collection

78
Silver rupee with a mint mark on the obverse and a leaf on the reverse

AD 1827/VS 1884
Authority: Ranjit Singh
Inscription: Nanakshahi couplet (as no. 1)

11.0g   23mm
1853,0606.45 Strachey collection

79
Silver rupee with a mint mark and numerals 95 on the obverse and a leaf on the reverse

AD 1827/VS 1884
Authority: Ranjit Singh
Inscription: Nanakshahi couplet (as no. 1)

11.1g   23mm
1912,0709.286 Bleazby collection

80
Silver rupee with a mint mark and numerals 95 on the obverse and a leaf on the reverse

AD 1827/VS 1884
Authority: Ranjit Singh
Inscription: Nanakshahi couplet (as no. 1)

11.2g   24mm
1936,1017.19 Baldwin collection

81
Silver rupee with a mint mark and numerals 96 on the obverse and a leaf on the reverse

AD 1827/VS 1884
Authority: Ranjit Singh
Inscription: Nanakshahi couplet (as no. 1)

11.1g   24mm
1912,0709.287 Bleazby collection

82
Silver rupee with a mint mark and numerals 97 on the obverse and a leaf on the reverse

AD 1827/VS 1884
Authority: Ranjit Singh
Inscription: Nanakshahi couplet (as no. 1)

11.1g   23mm
1936,1017.4 Baldwin collection

83
Silver rupee with a mint mark and numerals 97 on the obverse and a leaf on the reverse

AD 1827/VS 1884
Authority: Ranjit Singh
Inscription: Nanakshahi couplet (as no. 1)

11.1g   23mm
1912,0709.280 Bleazby collection

84
Silver rupee with a mint mark and numerals 97 on the obverse and a leaf on the reverse

AD 1827/VS 1884
Authority: Ranjit Singh
Inscription: Nanakshahi couplet (as no. 1)

11.1g   22mm
1936,1017.23 Baldwin collection

85
Silver rupee with a mint mark and numerals 99 on the obverse and a leaf on the reverse

AD 1827/VS 1884
Authority: Ranjit Singh
Inscription: Nanakshahi couplet (as no. 1)

11.1g   24mm
1936,1017.25 Baldwin collection

86
Silver rupee with a mint mark and numerals 99 on the obverse and a leaf on the reverse

AD 1827/VS 1884
Authority: Ranjit Singh
Inscription: Nanakshahi couplet (as no. 1)

11.0g   22mm
1912,0709.288 Bleazby collection

87
Silver rupee with a long stalked leaf on the obverse and a leaf on the reverse

AD 1827/VS 1884
Authority: Ranjit Singh
Inscription: Nanakshahi couplet (as no. 1)

11.0g   24mm
1936,1017.26 Baldwin collection

88
Silver rupee with a small punch dagger on the obverse and a leaf on the reverse

AD 1827/VS 1884
Authority: Ranjit Singh
Inscription: Nanakshahi couplet (as no. 1)

11.0g   24mm
1936,1017.30 Baldwin collection

89
Silver rupee with a leaf on the reverse

AD 1827/VS 1884
Authority: Ranjit Singh
Inscription: Nanakshahi couplet (as no. 1)

11.1g   23mm
1936,1017.27 Baldwin collection

Catalogue Nos 90–101

90
Silver rupee with a leaf on the reverse

AD 1827/VS 1884
Authority: Ranjit Singh
Inscription: Nanakshahi couplet (as no. 1)

10.1g   24mm
1912,0709.281 Bleazby collection

91
Silver rupee with a small flag and numerals 192 on the obverse and a leaf on the reverse

AD 1828/VS 1885
Authority: Ranjit Singh
Inscription: Nanakshahi couplet (as no. 1)

11.1g   23mm
1912,0709.290 Bleazby collection

92
Silver rupee with the word रम 'Ram' in Nagari on the obverse and a leaf on the reverse

AD 1828/VS 1885
Authority: Ranjit Singh
Inscription: Nanakshahi couplet (as no. 1)

11.0g   24mm
1903,1009.8 Talbot collection

93
Silver rupee with a mint mark and numerals 94 on the obverse and a leaf and small punch dagger on the reverse

AD 1828/VS 1885
Authority: Ranjit Singh
Inscription: Nanakshahi couplet (as no. 1)

11.2g   23mm
OR 5040

94
Silver rupee with the mint mark and numerals 95 on the obverse and a leaf on the reverse

AD 1828/VS 1885
Authority: Ranjit Singh
Inscription: Nanakshahi couplet (as no. 1)

11.1g   24mm
1874,1001.4 Guthrie collection

95
Silver rupee with the word ਸਤ 'Sat' meaning true in Gurmukhi, with a canopy above on the obverse and a leaf on the reverse

AD 1828/VS 1885
Authority: Ranjit Singh
Inscription: Nanakshahi couplet (as no. 1)

11.1g   25mm
OR 5041

96
Silver rupee with the word ओम 'Om', celestial sound in Nagri on the obverse and a leaf on the reverse

AD 1828/VS 1885
Authority: Ranjit Singh
Inscription: Nanakshahi couplet (as no. 1)

11.0g   23mm
1903,1009.6 Talbot collection

97
Silver rupee with flowers and the numerals 96 on the obverse and a leaf on the reverse

AD 1828/VS 1885
Authority: Ranjit Singh
Inscription: Nanakshahi couplet (as no. 1)

10.8g   23mm
1912,0709.291 Bleazby collection

98
Silver rupee with flowers on the obverse and a leaf on the reverse

AD 1828/VS 1885
Authority: Ranjit Singh
Inscription: Nanakshahi couplet (as no. 1)

10.8g   23mm
1887,0508.10 Theobald collection

99
Silver rupee with the word ओम 'Om' celestial sound in Nagri and numerals 97 on the obverse and a leaf on the reverse

AD 1828/VS 1885
Authority: Ranjit Singh
Inscription: Nanakshahi couplet (as no. 1)

11.1g   23mm
1874,1001.3 Guthrie collection

100
Silver rupee with the word ओम 'Om' celestial sound in Nagri and numerals 97 on the obverse and a leaf on the reverse

AD 1828/VS 1885
Authority: Ranjit Singh
Inscription: Nanakshahi couplet (as no. 1)

11.1g   23mm
1912,0709.294 Bleazby collection

101
Silver rupee with the word ओम 'Om' celestial sound in Nagri and numerals 97 on the obverse and a leaf on the reverse

AD 1828/VS 1885
Authority: Ranjit Singh
Inscription: Nanakshahi couplet (as no. 1)

11.1g   25mm
1912,0709.293 Bleazby collection

102
Silver rupee with the numerals 97 on the obverse and a leaf on the reverse

AD 1828/VS 1885
Authority: Ranjit Singh
Inscription: Nanakshahi couplet (as no. 1)

9.2g   22mm
1865,0803.70 Stubbs collection

103
Silver rupee with the word ओम 'Om' celestial sound in Nagri and numerals 97 on the obverse and a leaf on the reverse

AD 1828/VS 1885
Authority: Ranjit Singh
Inscription: Nanakshahi couplet (as no. 1)

11.1g   22mm
1912,0709.292 Bleazby collection

104
Silver rupee with a trident and numerals 97 on the obverse and a leaf on the reverse

AD 1828/VS 1885
Authority: Ranjit Singh
Inscription: Nanakshahi couplet (as no. 1)

11.0g   24mm
1912,0709.295 Bleazby collection

105
Silver rupee with a trident and numerals 98 on the obverse and a leaf on the reverse

AD 1828/VS 1885
Authority: Ranjit Singh
Inscription: Nanakshahi couplet (as no. 1)

11.1g   23mm
1936,1017.29 Baldwin collection

106
Silver rupee with an umbrella symbol and numerals 99 on the obverse and a leaf on the reverse

AD 1828/VS 1885
Authority: Ranjit Singh
Inscription: Nanakshahi couplet (as no. 1)

8.9g   23mm
1865,0803.71 Stubbs collection

107
Silver rupee with a trident and numerals 99 on the obverse and a leaf on the reverse

AD 1828/VS 1885
Authority: Ranjit Singh
Inscription: Nanakshahi couplet (as no. 1)

11.1g   22mm
1907,0702.18 Government of the Central Provinces of India

108
Silver rupee with an umbrella symbol on the obverse and a leaf on the reverse

AD 1828/VS 1885
Authority: Ranjit Singh
Inscription: Nanakshahi couplet (as no. 1)

11.1g   23mm
1936,1017.7 Baldwin collection

109
Silver rupee with umbrella symbol on the obverse and a leaf on the reverse

AD 1828/VS 1885
Authority: Ranjit Singh
Inscription: Nanakshahi couplet (as no. 1)

11.1g   23mm
1931,0809.4 Ingliss collection

110
Silver rupee with flag symbol on the obverse and numerals 193 and a leaf on the reverse

AD 1828/VS 1885
Authority: Ranjit Singh
Inscription: Nanakshahi couplet (as no. 1)

11.0g   23mm
1931,0809.2 Ingliss collection

111
Silver rupee with the word ਸਤ 'Sat' meaning true in Gurmukhi and numerals 193 on the obverse, and a leaf on the reverse

AD 1828/VS 1885
Authority: Ranjit Singh
Inscription: Nanakshahi couplet (as no. 1)

11.1g   23mm
1912,0709.299 Bleazby collection

112
Silver rupee with the word ਸਤ 'Sat' meaning true in Gurmukhi under a canopy on the obverse, and a leaf on the reverse

AD 1828/VS 1885
Authority: Ranjit Singh
Inscription: Nanakshahi couplet (as no. 1)

11.1g   24mm
1903,1009.7 Talbot collection

113
Silver rupee with the word ਸਤ 'Sat' meaning true in Gurmukhi under a canopy and a mint mark on the obverse and a leaf on the reverse

AD 1828/VS 1885
Authority: Ranjit Singh
Inscription: Nanakshahi couplet (as no. 1)

Catalogue Nos 114–124

11.1g 23mm
1912,0709.300 Bleazby collection

114

Silver rupee with the word ਸਤ 'Sat' meaning true in Gurmukhi under a canopy on the obverse, and a leaf on the reverse

AD 1828/VS 1885
Authority: Ranjit Singh
Inscription: Nanakshahi couplet (as no. 1)

11.1g 24mm
1936,1017.33 Baldwin collection

115

Silver rupee with an umbrella symbol and numerals 99 on the obverse and a leaf on the reverse

AD 1828/VS 1885
Authority: Ranjit Singh
Inscription: Nanakshahi couplet (as no. 1)

11.0g 23mm
1912,0709.296 Bleazby collection

116

Silver half rupee with a mint mark on the obverse and a leaf on the reverse

AD 1827/VS 1884
Authority: Ranjit Singh
Inscription: Nanakshahi couplet (as no. 1)

5.5g 20mm
1912,0709.274 Bleazby collection

117

Silver half rupee with a mint mark on the obverse and a leaf on the reverse

AD 1827/VS 1884
Authority: Ranjit Singh
Inscription: Nanakshahi couplet (as no. 1)

4.8g 19mm
1936,1017.20 Baldwin collection

118

Silver half rupee with a mint mark on the obverse and a leaf on the reverse

AD 1827/VS 1884
Authority: Ranjit Singh
Inscription: Nanakshahi couplet (as no. 1)

4.8g 18mm
1936,1017.28 Baldwin collection

119

Silver half rupee with an umbrella symbol and numerals 99 on the obverse and a leaf on the reverse

AD 1828/VS 1885
Authority: Ranjit Singh
Inscription: Nanakshahi couplet (as no. 1)

5.5g 20mm
1936,1017.31 Baldwin collection

120

Silver half rupee with flower symbol on the obverse and a leaf on the reverse

AD 1828/VS 1885
Authority: Ranjit Singh
Inscription: Nanakshahi couplet (as no. 1)

4.8g 17mm
1920,0514.77 Johnston collection

121

Silver half rupee with mint mark on the obverse and a leaf on the reverse

AD 1828/VS 1885
Authority: Ranjit Singh
Inscription: Nanakshahi couplet (as no. 1)

5.5g 19mm
OR 1720

122

Silver half rupee with the word ਸਤ 'Sat' meaning true in Gurmukhi and numerals 99 on the obverse and a leaf on the reverse

AD 1828/VS 1885
Authority: Ranjit Singh
Inscription: Nanakshahi couplet (as no. 1)

4.8g 18mm
1912,0709.297 Bleazby Collection

123

Silver half rupee with a mint mark and numerals 13 on the obverse and a leaf on the reverse

AD 1828/VS 1885
Authority: Ranjit Singh
Inscription: Nanakshahi couplet (as no. 1)

4.8g 18mm
1912,0709.282 Bleazby Collection

124

Silver half rupee with a mint mark and numerals 192 on the obverse and a leaf on the reverse

AD 1828/VS 1885
Authority: Ranjit Singh
Inscription: Nanakshahi couplet (as no. 1)

4.8g 18mm
1903,1009.11 Talbot Collection

125
Silver quarter rupee with an umbrella symbol on the obverse and a leaf on the reverse

AD 1828/VS 1885
Authority: Ranjit Singh
Inscription: Nanakshahi couplet (as no. 1)

2.7g   15mm
1920,0514.78 Johnston Collection

126
Silver quarter rupee with a mint mark on the obverse and a leaf on the reverse

AD 1828/VS 1885
Authority: Ranjit Singh
Inscription: Nanakshahi couplet (as no. 1)

2.7g   15mm
1912,0709.283 Bleazby Collection

127
Silver quarter rupee with an umbrella symbol and numerals 99 on the obverse and a leaf on the reverse

AD 1828/VS 1885
Authority: Ranjit Singh
Inscription: Nanakshahi couplet (as no. 1)

2.7g   17mm
1922,0424.2373 Whitehead Collection

128
Silver quarter rupee with a star flower on the obverse and a leaf on the reverse

AD 1828/VS 1885
Authority: Ranjit Singh
Inscription: Nanakshahi couplet (as no. 1)

2.6g   16mm
1912,0709.302 Bleazby collection

129
Silver quarter rupee with dot flowers on the obverse and a leaf on the reverse

AD 1828/VS 1885
Authority: Ranjit Singh
Inscription: Nanakshahi couplet (as no. 1)

2.7g   16mm
OR 1721

130
Silver quarter rupee with a mint mark and numerals 86 on the obverse and a leaf on the reverse

AD 1828/VS 1885
Authority: Ranjit Singh
Inscription: Nanakshahi couplet (as no. 1)

2.7g   15mm
1875,0502.120 Lincoln collection

131
Silver quarter rupee with dot patterns and numerals 94 on the obverse and a leaf on the reverse

AD 1828/VS 1885
Authority: Ranjit Singh
Inscription: Nanakshahi couplet (as no. 1)

2.6g   16mm
1912,0709.284 Bleazby collection

132
Silver quarter rupee with an umbrella symbol and numerals 99 on the obverse and a leaf on the reverse

AD 1828/VS 1885
Authority: Ranjit Singh
Inscription: Nanakshahi couplet (as no. 1)

2.8g   14mm
1912,0709.285 Bleazby collection

133
Silver quarter rupee with a star on the obverse and a leaf on the reverse

AD 1828/VS 1885
Authority: Ranjit Singh
Inscription: Nanakshahi couplet (as no. 1)

2.4g   14mm
1912,0709.303 Bleazby collection

134
Silver eighth of a rupee with a flower on the obverse and a leaf on the reverse

AD 1827/VS 1884
Authority: Ranjit Singh
Inscription: Nanakshahi couplet (as no. 1)

1.4g   12mm
1903,1009.12 Talbot collection

135
Silver eighth of a rupee with an umbrella symbol on the obverse and a leaf on the reverse

AD 1827/VS 1884
Authority: Ranjit Singh
Inscription: Nanakshahi couplet (as no. 1)

1.3g   12mm
1903,1009.9 Talbot collection

136
Silver eighth of a rupee with a mint mark and numerals 95 on the obverse and a leaf on the reverse

AD 1827/VS 1884
Authority: Ranjit Singh
Inscription: Nanakshahi couplet (as no. 1)

1.3g   13mm
1936,1017.22 Baldwin collection

Catalogue Nos 137–148

137

Silver eighth of a rupee with the word ਸਤ 'Sat' meaning true in Gurmukhi, with canopy above and numerals 95 on the obverse, and a leaf on the reverse

AD 1828/VS 1885
Authority: Ranjit Singh
Inscription: Nanakshahi couplet (as no. 1)

1.3g   13mm
1920,0514.79 Johnston collection

138

Silver eighth of a rupee with a mint mark and numerals 95 on the obverse and a leaf on the reverse

AD 1828/VS 1885
Authority: Ranjit Singh
Inscription: Nanakshahi couplet (as no. 1)

1.4g   13mm
OR 1722

139

Silver eighth of a rupee with the word ਸਤ 'Sat' meaning true in Gurmukhi, with canopy above on the obverse and a leaf on the reverse

AD 1828/VS 1885
Authority: Ranjit Singh
Inscription: Nanakshahi couplet (as no. 1)
1.3g   14mm
1912,0709.298 Bleazby collection

Copper coins

140

Copper hexagonal paisa with a leaf on the reverse

AD 1828/VS 1885
Authority: Ranjit Singh
Inscription: Gurmukhi (as no. 3)

17.7g   28mm
1912,0709.370 Bleazby collection

141

Copper paisa with a leaf on the reverse

AD 1828/VS 1885
Authority: Ranjit Singh
Inscription: Gurmukhi (as no. 3)

19.7g   27mm
1885,0610.51 C.J. Rodgers collection

142

Copper paisa with a leaf on the reverse

AD 1828/VS 1885
Authority: Ranjit Singh
Inscription: Gurmukhi (as no. 3)

28.9g   31mm
1885,0610.50 C.J. Rodgers collection

143

Copper paisa with a flower on the obverse and a leaf on the reverse

AD 1828/VS 1885
Authority: Ranjit Singh
Inscription: Gurmukhi (as no. 3)
28.8g   26mm
1912,0709.437 Bleazby collection

144

Copper paisa with a leaf on the reverse

AD 1828/VS 1885
Authority: Ranjit Singh
Inscription: Gurmukhi (as no. 3)

18.2g   27mm
1912,0709.371 Bleazby collection

145

Copper paisa with a leaf on the reverse

AD 1828/VS 1885
Authority: Ranjit Singh
Inscription: Gurmukhi (as no. 3)

19.0g   25mm
1912,0709.438 Bleazby collection

146

Copper paisa with a cross on the obverse and a leaf on the reverse

AD 1828/VS 1885
Authority: Ranjit Singh
Inscription: Gurmukhi (as no. 3)

12.0g   28mm
1912,0709.402 Bleazby collection

147

Copper paisa with a flower on the obverse and a leaf on the reverse

AD 1828/VS 1885
Authority: Ranjit Singh
Inscription: Gurmukhi (as no. 3)

10.4g   27mm
1912,0709.389 Bleazby collection

148

Copper paisa with a decorative edge on the obverse and a leaf on the reverse

AD 1828/VS 1885
Authority: Ranjit Singh
Inscription: Gurmukhi (as no. 3)

11.2g   22mm
1885,0610.53 C.J. Rodgers collection

149
Copper paisa with a leaf on the reverse

AD 1828/VS 1885
Authority: Ranjit Singh
Inscription: Gurmukhi (as no. 3)

10.8g 25mm
1885,0610.54 C.J. Rodgers collection

150
Copper paisa with a leaf on the reverse

AD 1828/VS 1885
Authority: Ranjit Singh
Inscription: Gurmukhi (as no. 3)

11.3g 22mm
1885,0610.52 C.J. Rodgers collection

151
Copper paisa with a leaf on the reverse

AD 1828/VS 1885
Authority: Ranjit Singh
Inscription: Gurmukhi (as no. 3)

11.3g 23mm
1903,1009.15 Talbot collection

152
Copper paisa with a leaf on the reverse

AD 1828/VS 1885
Authority: Ranjit Singh
Inscription: Gurmukhi (as no. 3)

11.3g 22mm
1903,1009.14 Talbot collection

153
Copper paisa with a leaf on the reverse

AD 1828/VS 1885
Authority: Ranjit Singh
Inscription: Gurmukhi (as no. 3)

11.2g 25mm
1912,0709.372 Bleazby collection

154
Copper paisa with a leaf on the reverse

AD 1828/VS 1885
Authority: Ranjit Singh
Inscription: Gurmukhi (as no. 3)

11.5g 23mm
1912,0709.419 Bleazby collection

155
Copper paisa with a leaf on the reverse

AD 1828/VS 1885
Authority: Ranjit Singh
Inscription: Gurmukhi (as no. 3)

11.3g 23mm
1912,0709.394 Bleazby collection

156
Copper paisa with a leaf on the reverse

AD 1828/VS 1885
Authority: Ranjit Singh
Inscription: Gurmukhi (as no. 3)

11.2g 23mm
1912,0709.403 Bleazby collection

157
Copper paisa with a leaf on the reverse

AD 1828/VS 1885
Authority: Ranjit Singh
Inscription: Gurmukhi (as no. 3)

12.0g 23mm
1912,0709.443 Bleazby collection

158
Double copper paisa with a leaf on the reverse

AD 1828/VS 1885
Authority: Ranjit Singh
Inscription: Gurmukhi (as no. 3)

10.9g 22mm
1903,1009.17 Talbot collection

159
Double copper paisa with a leaf on the reverse

AD 1828/VS 1885
Authority: Ranjit Singh
Inscription: Gurmukhi (as no. 3)

11.2g 22mm
1912,0709.444 Bleazby collection

160
Double copper paisa with a leaf on the reverse

AD 1828/VS 1885
Authority: Ranjit Singh
Inscription: Gurmukhi (as no. 3)

11.0g 24mm
1912,0709.418 Bleazby collection

Catalogue Nos 161–172

161
Double copper paisa with a leaf on the reverse

AD 1828/VS 1885
Authority: Ranjit Singh
Inscription: Gurmukhi (as no. 3)

11.2g   21mm
1912,0709.373 Bleazby collection

162
Double copper paisa with a leaf on the reverse

AD 1828/VS 1885
Authority: Ranjit Singh
Inscription: Gurmukhi (as no. 3)

11.1g   23mm
1912,0709.374 Bleazby collection

163
Double copper paisa with a cross on the obverse and a leaf on the reverse

AD 1828/VS 1885
Authority: Ranjit Singh
Inscription: Gurmukhi (as no. 3)

11.8g   23mm
1903,1009.27 Talbot collection

164
Double copper paisa with a leaf on the reverse

AD 1828/VS 1885
Authority: Ranjit Singh
Inscription: Gurmukhi (as no. 3)

11.6g   20mm
1912,0709.397 Bleazby collection

165
Copper half-paisa with a flower on the obverse and a leaf on the reverse

AD 1828/VS 1885
Authority: Ranjit Singh
Inscription: Gurmukhi (as no. 3)

6.9g   21mm
OR 5044

166
Double copper paisa with a leaf on the reverse

AD 1828/VS 1885
Authority: Ranjit Singh
Inscription: Gurmukhi (as no. 3)

11.1g   21mm
1912,0709.393 Bleazby collection

167
Double copper paisa (double-struck) with a leaf on the reverse

AD 1828/VS 1885
Authority: Ranjit Singh
Inscription: Gurmukhi (as no. 3)

11.3g   24mm
1912,0709.400 Bleazby collection

168
Double copper paisa with a leaf on the reverse

AD 1828/VS 1885
Authority: Ranjit Singh
Inscription: Gurmukhi (as no. 3)

11.2g   23mm
1912,0709.376 Bleazby collection

169
Double copper paisa with a leaf on the reverse

AD 1828/VS 1885
Authority: Ranjit Singh
Inscription: Gurmukhi (as no. 3)

11.1g   23mm
1912,0709.377 Bleazby collection

170
Double copper paisa with a leaf on the reverse

AD 1828/VS 1885
Authority: Ranjit Singh
Inscription: Gurmukhi (as no. 3)

11.2g   23mm
1912,0709.378 Bleazby collection

171
Copper paisa with a leaf on the reverse

AD 1828/VS 1885
Authority: Ranjit Singh
Inscription: Gurmukhi (as no. 3)

11.3g   21mm
1912,0709.379 Bleazby collection

172
Copper square paisa/anna with a leaf on the reverse

AD 1828/VS 1885
Authority: Ranjit Singh
Inscription: Gurmukhi (as no. 3)

31.7g   22mm
1912,0709.380 Bleazby collection

173
Copper paisa with a leaf on the reverse

AD 1828/VS 1885
Authority: Ranjit Singh
Inscription: Gurmukhi (as no. 3)

11.3g 22mm
1912,0709.381 Bleazby collection

174
Copper paisa with a leaf on the reverse

AD 1828/VS 1885
Authority: Ranjit Singh
Inscription: Gurmukhi (as no. 3)

11.4g 23mm
1912,0709.382 Bleazby collection

175
Copper paisa with a leaf on the reverse

AD 1828/VS 1885
Authority: Ranjit Singh
Inscription: Gurmukhi (as no. 3)

11.0g 22mm
1912,0709.384 Bleazby collection

176
Copper paisa with a leaf on the reverse

AD 1828/VS 1885
Authority: Ranjit Singh
Inscription: Gurmukhi (as no. 3)

11.2g 24mm
1912,0709.383 Bleazby collection

177
Copper paisa with a leaf on the reverse

AD 1828/VS 1885
Authority: Ranjit Singh
Inscription: Gurmukhi (as no. 3)

11.4g 23mm
1912,0709.387 Bleazby collection

178
Copper paisa with a leaf on the reverse

AD 1828/VS 1885
Authority: Ranjit Singh
Inscription: Gurmukhi (as no. 3)

11.1g 22mm
1912,0709.388 Bleazby collection

179
Copper paisa with a leaf on the reverse

AD 1828/VS 1885
Authority: Ranjit Singh
Inscription: Gurmukhi (as no. 3)

11.1g 24mm
1912,0709.445 Bleazby collection

180
Copper paisa with a leaf on the reverse

AD 1828/VS 1885
Authority: Ranjit Singh
Inscription: Gurmukhi (as no. 3)

11.0g 24mm
1912,0709.385 Bleazby collection

181
Copper paisa with a leaf on the reverse

AD 1828/VS 1885
Authority: Ranjit Singh
Inscription: Gurmukhi (as no. 3)

11.2g 23mm
1912,0709.390 Bleazby collection

182
Copper paisa with a leaf on the reverse

AD 1828/VS 1885
Authority: Ranjit Singh
Inscription: Gurmukhi (as no. 3)

11.4g 22mm
1912,0709.391 Bleazby collection

183
Copper paisa with a leaf on the reverse

AD 1828/VS 1885
Authority: Ranjit Singh
Inscription: Gurmukhi (as no. 3)

11.4g 23mm
1912,0709.416 Bleazby collection

184
Copper paisa with a leaf on the reverse

AD 1828/VS 1885
Authority: Ranjit Singh
Inscription: Gurmukhi (as no. 3)

11.8g 22mm
1912,0709.417 Bleazby collection

Catalogue Nos 185–196

185
Copper paisa with a leaf on the reverse

AD 1828/VS 1885
Authority: Ranjit Singh
Inscription: Gurmukhi (as no. 3)

11.0g 22mm
1912,0709.412 Bleazby collection

186
Copper paisa with a cross symbol on the obverse and a leaf on the reverse

AD 1828/VS 1885
Authority: Ranjit Singh
Inscription: Gurmukhi (as no. 3)

12.0g 24mm
1912,0709.415 Bleazby collection

187
Copper paisa with a leaf on the reverse

AD 1828/VS 1885
Authority: Ranjit Singh
Inscription: Gurmukhi (as no. 3)

11.1g 21mm
1912,0709.420 Bleazby collection

188
Copper paisa with a leaf on the reverse

AD 1828/VS 1885
Authority: Ranjit Singh
Inscription: Gurmukhi (as no. 3)

9.4g 22mm
1912,0709.422 Bleazby collection

189
Copper paisa with a leaf on the reverse

AD 1828/VS 1885
Authority: Ranjit Singh
Inscription: Gurmukhi (as no. 3)

11.2g 21mm
1912,0709.423 Bleazby collection

190
Copper paisa with a leaf on the reverse

AD 1828/VS 1885
Authority: Ranjit Singh
Inscription: Gurmukhi (as no. 3)

11.2g 22mm
1903,1009.19 Talbot collection

191
Copper paisa with a leaf on the reverse

AD 1828/VS 1885
Authority: Ranjit Singh
Inscription: Gurmukhi (as no. 3)

10.2g 20mm
1912,0709.425 Bleazby collection

192
Copper paisa with a leaf on the reverse

AD 1828/VS 1885
Authority: Ranjit Singh
Inscription: Gurmukhi (as no. 3)

12.0g 24mm
1903,1009.22 Talbot collection

193
Copper paisa with a leaf on the reverse

AD 1828/VS 1885
Authority: Ranjit Singh
Inscription: Gurmukhi (as no. 3)

10.9g 24mm
1912,0709.424 Bleazby collection

194
Copper paisa with a leaf on the reverse

AD 1828/VS 1885
Authority: Ranjit Singh
Inscription: Gurmukhi (as no. 3)

11.0g 21mm
1912,0709.426 Bleazby collection

195
Copper paisa with a leaf on the reverse

AD 1828/VS 1885
Authority: Ranjit Singh
Inscription: Gurmukhi (as no. 3)

9.6g 22mm
1912,0709.427 Bleazby collection

196
Copper paisa with a leaf on the reverse

AD 1828/VS 1885
Authority: Ranjit Singh
Inscription: Gurmukhi (as no. 3)

8.4g 19mm
1912,0709.428 Bleazby collection

Catalogue Nos 197–207

197
Copper paisa with a leaf on the reverse

AD 1828/VS 1885
Authority: Ranjit Singh
Inscription: Gurmukhi (as no. 3)

8.4g   21mm
1912,0709.429 Bleazby collection

198
Copper paisa with a leaf on the reverse

AD 1828/VS 1885
Authority: Ranjit Singh

Obverse: Gurmukhi and Persian
ਅਕਾਲ ਸਹਾਇ ਗੁਰੂ ਨਾਨਕ ਜੀ
دیوکی

Transliteration
Akal Sahai Guru Nanak Ji
Devaki

Translation
The immortal Lord (akaal) helps the illustrious Guru Nanak
Devaki [name of the Wife of Vasudeva and Lord Krishna's Mother]

Reverse: Gurmukhi
ਜਰਬ ਸਰੀ ਅੰਬ ਰਤਸਰ ਜੀ ੧੮੮੫

Transliteration
Zarb Sri Amritsar Ji 1885

Translation
Struck at the illustrious Amritsar in VS 1885

7.0g   20mm
1903,1009.55 Talbot collection

199
Copper paisa with a leaf on the reverse

AD 1828/VS 1885
Authority: Ranjit Singh
Inscription: (as no. 198)

7.2g   20mm
1903,1009.57 Talbot collection

200
Copper paisa with a leaf on the reverse

AD 1828/VS 1885
Authority: Ranjit Singh
Inscription: (as no. 198)

6.9g   20mm
1903,1009.53 Talbot collection

201
Copper paisa with a leaf on the reverse

AD 1828/VS 1885
Authority: Ranjit Singh
Inscription: (as no. 198)

6.9g   19mm
1885,0610.59 C.J. Rodgers collection

202
Copper paisa with a flag on the obverse and a leaf on the reverse

AD 1828/VS 1885
Authority: Ranjit Singh
Inscription: (as no. 3)

8.6g   21mm
1903,1009.37 Talbot collection

203
Copper paisa with a flag on the obverse and a leaf on the reverse

AD 1828/VS 1885
Authority: Ranjit Singh
Inscription: (as no. 3)

8.6g   21mm
1903,1009.34 Talbot collection

204
Copper paisa with a flag on the obverse and a leaf on the reverse

AD 1828/VS 1885
Authority: Ranjit Singh
Inscription: (as no. 3)

8.6g   21mm
1903,1009.36 Talbot collection

205
Copper paisa with a flag on the obverse and a leaf on the reverse

AD 1828/VS 1885
Authority: Ranjit Singh
Inscription: (as no. 3)

8.2g   21mm
1903,1009.35 Talbot collection

206
Copper paisa with a leaf on the reverse

AD 1828/VS 1885
Authority: Ranjit Singh
Inscription: (as no. 3)

11.1g   21mm
1903,1009.44 Talbot collection

207
Copper paisa with a leaf on the reverse

AD 1828/VS 1885
Authority: Ranjit Singh
Inscription: (as no. 3)

11.0g   26mm
1912,0709.392 Bleazby collection

Catalogue Nos 208–219

208
Copper paisa with a leaf on the reverse

AD 1828/VS 1885
Authority: Ranjit Singh
Inscription: (as no. 3)

11.1g 23mm
1903,1009.21 Talbot collection

209
Copper paisa with a leaf on the reverse

AD 1828/VS 1885
Authority: Ranjit Singh
Inscription: (as no. 3)

11.4g 23mm
1903,1009.20 Talbot collection

210
Copper paisa with a leaf on the reverse

AD 1828/VS 1885
Authority: Ranjit Singh
Inscription: (as no. 3)

11.2g 22mm
1903,1009.23 Talbot collection

211
Copper paisa with a leaf on the reverse

AD 1828/VS 1885
Authority: Ranjit Singh
Inscription: (as no. 3)

11.4g 21mm
1903,1009.24 Talbot collection

212
Copper paisa with a leaf on the reverse

AD 1828/VS 1885
Authority: Ranjit Singh
Inscription: (as no. 3)

11.3g 22mm
1903,1009.25 Talbot collection

213
Copper paisa with a leaf on the reverse

AD 1828/VS 1885
Authority: Ranjit Singh
Inscription: (as no. 3)

11.2g 23mm
1903,1009.26 Talbot collection

214
Copper paisa with a leaf on the reverse

AD 1828/VS 1885
Authority: Ranjit Singh
Inscription: (as no. 3)

9.6g 20mm
1912,0709.434 Bleazby collection

215
Copper paisa with a leaf on the reverse

AD 1828/VS 1885
Authority: Ranjit Singh
Inscription: (as no. 3)

11.2g 22mm
1912,0709.406 Bleazby collection

216
Copper paisa with a leaf on the reverse

AD 1828/VS 1885
Authority: Ranjit Singh
Inscription: (as no. 3)

11.4g 23mm
1912,0709.407 Bleazby collection

217
Copper paisa with a small cross on the obverse and a leaf on the reverse

AD 1828/VS 1885
Authority: Ranjit Singh
Inscription: (as no. 3)

10.1g 20mm
1912,0709.410 Bleazby collection

218
Copper paisa with a leaf on the reverse

AD 1828/VS 1885
Authority: Ranjit Singh
Inscription: (as no. 3)

11.1g 20mm
1912,0709.411 Bleazby collection

219
Copper paisa with a leaf on the reverse

AD 1828/VS 1885
Authority: Ranjit Singh
Inscription: (as no. 3)

11.0g 27mm
1912,0709.401 Bleazby collection

Catalogue Nos 220–231

220
Copper paisa with a leaf on the reverse

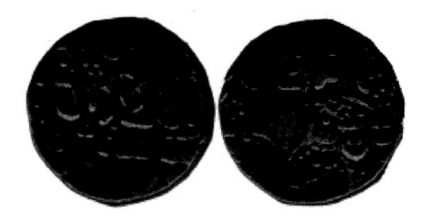

AD 1828/VS 1885
Authority: Ranjit Singh
Inscription: (as no. 3)

11.8g   24mm
1912,0709.408 Bleazby collection

221
Copper paisa with a leaf on the reverse

AD 1828/VS 1885
Authority: Ranjit Singh
Inscription: (as no. 3)

11.3g   22mm
1912,0709.413 Bleazby collection

222
Copper paisa with a leaf on the reverse

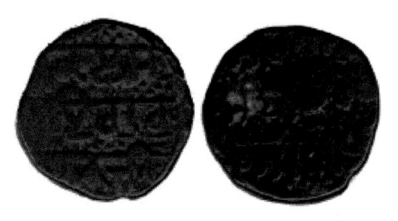

AD 1828/VS 1885
Authority: Ranjit Singh
Inscription: (as no. 3)

11.3g   22mm
1903,1009.18 Talbot collection

223
Copper paisa with a leaf on the reverse

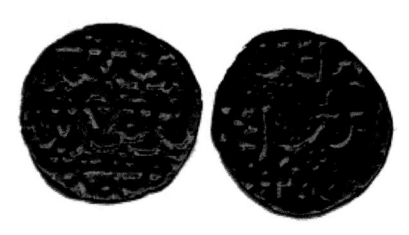

AD 1828/VS 1885
Authority: Ranjit Singh
Inscription: (as no. 3)

11.2g   23mm
1912,0709.395 Bleazby collection

224
Copper paisa with a star on the obverse and a leaf on the reverse

AD 1828/VS 1885
Authority: Ranjit Singh
Inscription: (as no. 3)

10.4g   26mm
1912,0709.396 Bleazby collection

225
Copper paisa with a leaf on the reverse

AD 1828/VS 1885
Authority: Ranjit Singh
Inscription: (as no. 3)

11.3g   21mm
1912,0709.404 Bleazby collection

226
Copper paisa with a leaf on the reverse

AD 1828/VS 1885
Authority: Ranjit Singh
Inscription: (as no. 3)

11.4g   21mm
1912,0709.398 Bleazby collection

227
Copper paisa with a leaf on the reverse

AD 1828/VS 1885
Authority: Ranjit Singh
Inscription: (as no. 3)

11.4g   22mm
1912,0709.399 Bleazby collection

228
Copper paisa with a leaf on the reverse

AD 1828/VS 1885
Authority: Ranjit Singh
Inscription: (as no. 3)

11.4g   22mm
1903,1009.16 Talbot collection

229
Copper paisa with a leaf on the reverse

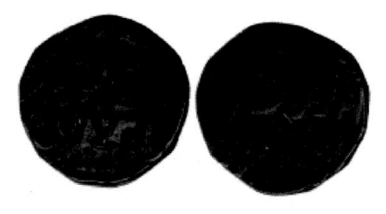

AD 1828/VS 1885
Authority: Ranjit Singh
Inscription: (as no. 3)

11.3g   22mm
1912,0709.386 Bleazby collection

230
Copper paisa with a tiger on the obverse and a leaf on the reverse

AD 1828/VS 1885
[The tiger on the obverse may refer to the reign of Maharaja Sher Singh, however the date remains frozen on this coin 1885 (vs)]
Authority: Ranjit Singh
Inscription: (as no. 3)

9.6g   20mm
1912,0709.441 Bleazby collection

231
Copper paisa with a tiger on the obverse and a leaf on the reverse

AD 1828/VS 1885
Authority: Ranjit Singh
Inscription: (as no. 3)

9.5g   20mm
1912,0709.442 Bleazby collection

Catalogue Nos 232–243

232
Copper paisa with a tiger on the obverse and a leaf on the reverse

AD 1828/VS 1885
Authority: Ranjit Singh
Inscription: (as no. 3)

9.6g 21mm
1912,0709.440 Bleazby collection

233
Copper paisa with a leaf on the reverse

AD 1828/VS 1885
Authority: Ranjit Singh
Inscription: (as no. 3)

11.1g 21mm
1912,0709.386 Bleazby collection

234
Copper paisa with a leaf on the reverse

AD 1828/VS 1885
Authority: Ranjit Singh
Inscription: (as no. 3)

11.5g 22mm
1912,0709.401.a Bleazby collection

235
Copper double struck paisa with a leaf on the reverse

AD 1828/VS 1885
Authority: Ranjit Singh
Inscription: (as no. 3)

8.5g 24mm
1903,1009.59 Talbot collection

236
Copper double struck paisa with a leaf on the reverse

AD 1828/VS 1885
Authority: Ranjit Singh
Inscription: (as no. 3)

8.4g 22mm
1903,1009.60 Talbot collection

237
Copper paisa with a leaf on the reverse

AD 1828/VS 1885
Authority: Ranjit Singh
Inscription: (as no. 3)

10.1g 20mm
OR 1725

238
Copper paisa with a leaf on the reverse

AD 1828/VS 1885
Authority: Ranjit Singh
Inscription: (as no. 3)

11.2g 20mm
OR 1728

239
Copper paisa with a leaf on the reverse

AD 1828/VS 1885
Authority: Ranjit Singh
Inscription: (as no. 3)

11.2g 24mm
1870,0507.13059 Freudenthal collection

240
Copper paisa with a leaf on the reverse

AD 1828/VS 1885
Authority: Ranjit Singh
Inscription: (as no. 3)

11.4g 22mm
1860,1220.593 Major Hay collection

241
Copper paisa with a leaf on the reverse

AD 1828/VS 1885
Authority: Ranjit Singh
Inscription: (as no. 3)

10.9g 22mm
1859,0220.124 Brind collection

242
Copper paisa with a leaf on the reverse

AD 1828/VS 1885
Authority: Ranjit Singh
Inscription: (as no. 3)

11.0g 21mm
1859,0220.118 Brind collection

243
Copper paisa with a punch dagger on the obverse and a leaf on the reverse

AD 1828/VS 1885
Authority: Ranjit Singh
Inscription: (as no. 3)

8.6g 19mm
1860,1220.594 Hay collection

Catalogue Nos 244–255

244
Copper paisa with a leaf on the reverse

AD 1828/VS 1885
Authority: Ranjit Singh
Inscription: (as no. 3)

11.4g 22mm
OR 5045

245
Copper paisa with a leaf on the reverse

AD 1828/VS 1885
Authority: Ranjit Singh
Inscription: (as no. 3)

10.9g 21mm
1870,0507.13061 Freudenthal collection

246
Copper paisa with a punch dagger on the obverse and a leaf on the reverse

AD 1828/VS 1885
Authority: Ranjit Singh
Inscription: (as no. 3)

9.4g 20mm
1859,0220.117 Brind collection

247
Copper paisa with a punch dagger on the obverse and a leaf on the reverse

AD 1828/VS 1885
Authority: Ranjit Singh
Inscription: (as no. 3)

9.4g 21mm
1859,0220.116 Brind collection

248
Copper paisa with a punch dagger on the obverse and a leaf on the reverse

AD 1828/VS 1885
Authority: Ranjit Singh
Inscription: (as no. 3)

9.5g 22mm
OR 1730

249
Copper paisa with a leaf on the reverse

AD 1828/VS 1885
Authority: Ranjit Singh
Inscription: (as no. 3)

9.5g 22mm
1859,0220.122 Brind collection

250
Copper paisa with a punch dagger on the obverse and a leaf on the reverse

AD 1828/VS 1885
Authority: Ranjit Singh
Inscription: (as no. 3)

9.3g 21mm
1859,0220.119 Brind collection

251
Copper paisa with a punch dagger on the obverse and a leaf on the reverse

AD 1828/VS 1885
Authority: Ranjit Singh
Inscription: (as no. 3)

9.3g 21mm
1859,0220.120 Brind collection

252
Copper paisa with a leaf on the reverse

AD 1828/VS 1885
Authority: Ranjit Singh
Inscription: (as no. 3)

10.7g 20mm
1859,0220.121 Brind collection

253
Copper paisa with a star symbol on the obverse and a leaf on the reverse

AD 1828/VS 1885
Authority: Ranjit Singh
Inscription: (as no. 3)

10.3g 21mm
1859,0220.123 Brind collection

254
Copper paisa with a leaf on the reverse

AD 1828/VS 1885
Authority: Ranjit Singh
Inscription: (as no. 3)

8.3g 19mm
1870,0507.13060 Freudenthal collection

255
Copper paisa with a leaf on the reverse

AD 1823/VS 1880
Authority: Ranjit Singh
Inscription: Gobindshahi couplet

Obverse: Persian

دیگ و تیغ و فتح نصرت بیدرنگ یافت از نانک
گورگوبند سنگ

Transliteration
Deg o tegh o fath nusrat bedrang Yaft az Nanak Gur Gobind Singh

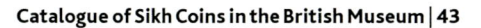

Catalogue Nos 256–266

Translation
Abundance, power and victory [and] assistance without delay, are the gifts of Nanak [and] Guru Gobind Singh

Reverse: Persian

سری امرتسر سنا جلوس ضرب میمنت مانوس

Transliteration
Sri Amritsar Sanah Julus zarb maimanat manus

Translation
Struck at the illustrious Amritsar In the year of the prosperous human reign

10.7g   20mm
1870,0507.13294 Freudenthal collection

256
Copper paisa with a leaf on the reverse

AD 1809/VS 1866
Authority: Ranjit Singh
Inscription: Gobindshahi couplet (as no. 255)

9.3g   22mm
1912,0709.340 Bleazby collection

257
Copper paisa with a leaf on the reverse

AD 1813/VS 1870
Authority: Ranjit Singh
Inscription: Gobindshahi couplet (as no. 255)

10.9g   21mm
1903,1009.39 Talbot collection

258
Copper paisa with a leaf on the reverse

AD 1823/VS 1880
Authority: Ranjit Singh
Inscription: Gobindshahi couplet (as no. 255)
The engraver has incorrectly used the coin dye as a mirror image therefore the inscription appears backwards on the obverse

10.9g   20mm
1903,1009.63 Talbot collection

259
Copper paisa with a leaf on the reverse

AD 1823/VS 1880
Authority: Ranjit Singh
Inscription: Gobindshahi couplet (as no. 255)

11.4g   22mm
1903,1009.64 Talbot collection

260
Copper paisa with a mint mark on the obverse and a leaf on the reverse

AD 1819/VS 1876
Authority: Ranjit Singh
Inscription: Gobindshahi couplet (as no. 255)

9.8g   22mm
1912,0709.341 Bleazby collection

261
Copper square paisa with a mint mark on the obverse and a leaf on the reverse

AD 1820/VS 1877
Authority: Ranjit Singh
Inscription: Gobindshahi couplet (as no. 255)

11.1g   18 x 17mm
1912,0709.342 Bleazby collection

262
Copper octagonal paisa with a star on the obverse and a leaf on the reverse

AD 1821/VS 1878
Authority: Ranjit Singh
Inscription: Gobindshahi couplet (as no. 255)

11.0g   22mm
1912,0709.343 Bleazby collection

263
Copper hexagonal paisa with a star on the obverse and a leaf on the reverse

AD 1822/VS 1879
Authority: Ranjit Singh
Inscription: Gobindshahi couplet (as no. 255)

11.0g   21 x 23mm
1912,0709.344 Bleazby collection

264
Copper paisa with a leaf on the reverse

AD 1823/VS 1880
Authority: Ranjit Singh
Inscription: Gobindshahi couplet (as no. 255)

9.6g   23mm
1912,0709.345 Bleazby collection

265
Copper paisa with a leaf on the reverse

AD 1823/VS 1880
Authority: Ranjit Singh
Inscription: Gobindshahi couplet (as no. 255)

11.8g   24mm
1912,0709.346 Bleazby collection

266
Copper paisa with a leaf on the obverse and a flower on the reverse

AD 1823/VS 1880
Authority: Ranjit Singh
Inscription: Gobindshahi couplet (as no. 255)

11.5g   23mm
1912,0709.347 Bleazby collection

Catalogue Nos 267–278

267

Copper paisa with a leaf on the obverse and a flower on the reverse

AD 1823/VS 1880
Authority: Ranjit Singh
Inscription: Gobindshahi couplet (as no. 255)

11.3g   22mm
1912,0709.349 Bleazby collection

268

Copper paisa with a leaf on the obverse and a flower on the reverse

AD 1823/VS 1880
Authority: Ranjit Singh
Inscription: Gobindshahi couplet (as no. 255)

11.5g   23mm
1912,0709.348 Bleazby collection

269

Copper paisa with a leaf on the obverse and a flower on the reverse

AD 1823/VS 1880
Authority: Ranjit Singh
Inscription: Gobindshahi couplet (as no. 255)

11.7g   25mm
1912,0709.350 Bleazby collection

270

Copper paisa with a leaf on the obverse and a flower on the reverse

AD 1823/VS 1880
Authority: Ranjit Singh
Inscription: Gobindshahi couplet (as no. 255)

11.7g   22mm
OR 5046

271

Copper paisa with a leaf on the reverse

AD 1823/VS 1880
Authority: Ranjit Singh
Inscription: Gobindshahi couplet (as no. 255)

11.8g   22mm
1865,0803.72 Stubbs collection

272

Copper paisa with a leaf on the obverse and a flower on the reverse

AD 1823/VS 1880
Authority: Ranjit Singh
Inscription: Gobindshahi couplet (as no. 255)

11.8g   24mm
1885,0610.47 C.J. Rodgers collection

273

Copper paisa with a leaf on the reverse

AD 1823/VS 1880
Authority: Ranjit Singh
Inscription: Gobindshahi couplet (as no. 255)

11.8g   22mm
OR 5048

274

Copper paisa with a leaf on the reverse

AD 1824/VS 1881
Authority: Ranjit Singh
Inscription: Gobindshahi couplet (as no. 255)

10.6g   21mm
1912,0709.355 Bleazby collection

275

Copper paisa with a leaf on the reverse

AD 1824/VS 1881
Authority: Ranjit Singh
Inscription: Gobindshahi couplet (as no. 255)

11.1g   22mm
1912,0709.353 Bleazby collection

276

Copper paisa with a leaf on the reverse

AD 1824/VS 1881
Authority: Ranjit Singh
Inscription: Gobindshahi couplet (as no. 255)

11.9g   22mm
1912,0709.354 Bleazby collection

277

Copper paisa with a leaf on the reverse

AD 1824/VS 1881
Authority: Ranjit Singh
Inscription: Gobindshahi couplet (as no. 255)

11.5g   23mm
1870,0507.13295 Freudenthal collection

278

Copper paisa with a leaf on the reverse

AD 1824/VS 1881
Authority: Ranjit Singh
Inscription: Gobindshahi couplet (as no. 255)

11.5g   21mm
1903,1009.40 Talbot collection

279
Copper paisa with a leaf on the reverse

AD 1825/VS 1882
Authority: Ranjit Singh
Inscription: Gobindshahi couplet (as no. 255)

11.5g 21mm
1903,1009.38 Talbot collection

280
Copper paisa with a trident on the obverse and a leaf on the reverse

AD 1828/VS 1885
Authority: Ranjit Singh
Inscription: Gobindshahi couplet (as no. 255)

10.0g 22mm
1912,0709.360 Bleazby collection

281
Copper paisa with a leaf on the reverse

AD 1828/VS 1885
Authority: Ranjit Singh
Inscription: Gobindshahi couplet (as no. 255)

10.1g 21mm
1912,0709.358 Bleazby collection

282
Copper paisa with a leaf on the reverse

AD 1829/VS 1886
Authority: Ranjit Singh
Inscription: Gobindshahi couplet (as no. 255)

10.6g 20mm
1912,0709.359 Bleazby collection

283
Copper paisa with a leaf on the obverse and the numerals 94 on the reverse

AD 1828/VS 1885
Authority: Ranjit Singh
Inscription: Gobindshahi couplet (as no. 255)

15.7g 25mm
1885,0610.49 C.J. Rodgers collection

284
Copper square paisa with a leaf on the reverse

AD 1824/VS 1881
Authority: Ranjit Singh
Inscription: Gobindshahi couplet (as no. 255)

11.6g 11 x 11mm
1912,0709.361 Bleazby collection

285
Copper paisa with a leaf on the reverse

AD 1828/VS 1885
Authority: Ranjit Singh
Inscription: (as no. 3)

7.9g 21mm
1902,0608.335 Hoernle collection

286
Copper paisa with a leaf on the reverse

AD 1828/VS 1885
Authority: Ranjit Singh
Inscription: (as no. 198)

6.9g 19mm
1903,1009.54 Talbot collection

287
Copper paisa with a punch dagger on the obverse and a leaf on the reverse

AD 1840/VS 1897
Authority: Kharak Singh

Obverse: Gumukhi

ਅਕਾਲ ਸਹਾਇ ਗੁਰੂ ਨਾਨਕ ਜੀ

Transliteration
Akal Sahai Guru Nanak Ji

Translation
The Lord (akal) helps the illustrious Guru Nanak

Reverse: Persian

جلوس میمنت مانوس ضرب سری امرتسر سنه

Transliteration
Julus maimanut manus, Zarb Sri Amritsar Sanah

Translation
Struck in Amritsar in the illustrious year of the human reign

10.8g 21mm
1903,1009.32 Talbot collection

288
Copper paisa with a leaf on the reverse

Obverse: (as no. 15)

Reverse: date and inscription illegible

10.6g 21mm
1903,1009.66 Talbot collection

289
Copper double struck paisa with a leaf on the reverse

AD 1828/VS 1885
Authority: Ranjit Singh
Inscription: (as no. 3)

18.4g 32mm
1865,0802.67 Bush collection

290
Copper square paisa with a leaf on the reverse

AD 1828/VS 1885
Authority: Ranjit Singh
Inscription: (as no. 3)

42.2g   24 x 24mm
1885,0610.55 C.J. Rodgers collection

291
Copper half paisa with a leaf on the reverse

AD 1828/VS 1885
Authority: Ranjit Singh

Obverse: Gumukhi
ਅਕਾਲ ਦੇਵਕੀ ਨਾਮਦਨਜੀ

Transliteration
Akal Devaki Namdanaji

Translation
Immortal mother of Lord Krishna [Namdana is one of many names of Lord Krishna]

Reverse: Gurmukhi
ਜਰਬ ਸਰੀ ਅੰਬ ਰਤਸਰ ਜੀ ੧੮੮੫

Transliteration
Zarb Sri Amritsar Ji 1885

Translation
Struck at the illustrious Amritsar in VS 1885

6.9g   18mm
1903,1009.46 Talbot collection

292
Copper half paisa with a leaf on the reverse

AD 1828/VS 1885
Authority: Ranjit Singh
Inscription: (as no. 291)

6.9g   19mm
1903,1009.49 Talbot collection

293
Copper half paisa with a leaf on the reverse

AD 1828/VS 1885
Authority: Ranjit Singh
Inscription: (as no. 291)

6.7g   20mm
1903,1009.47 Talbot collection

294
Copper half paisa with a leaf on the reverse

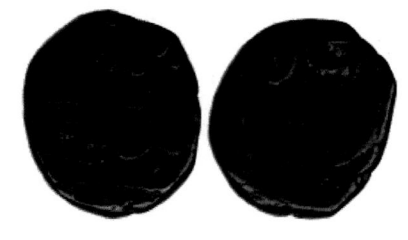

AD 1828/VS 1885
Authority: Ranjit Singh
Inscription: (as no. 291)

6.7g   19mm
1903,1009.48 Talbot collection

295
Copper half paisa with a leaf on the reverse

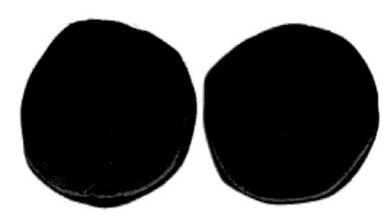

AD 1828/VS 1885
Authority: Ranjit Singh
Inscription: (as no. 291)

6.7g   19mm
1903,1009.50 Talbot collection

296
Copper half paisa with a leaf on the reverse

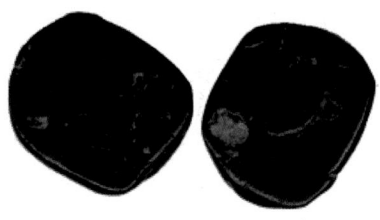

AD 1828/VS 1885
Authority: Ranjit Singh
Inscription: (as no. 291)

6.6g   20mm
1903,1009.51 Talbot collection

297
Copper half paisa with a leaf on the reverse

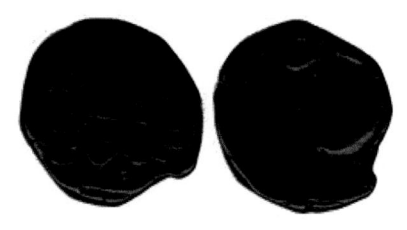

AD 1828/VS 1885
Authority: Ranjit Singh
Inscription: (as no. 291)

6.7g   21mm
1903,1009.52 Talbot collection

298
Copper half paisa with punch dagger on the obverse and a leaf on the reverse

AD 1828/VS 1885
Authority: Ranjit Singh
Inscription: (as no. 3)

8.6g   20mm
1903,1009.33 Talbot collection

299
Copper half paisa with punch dagger on the obverse and a leaf on the reverse

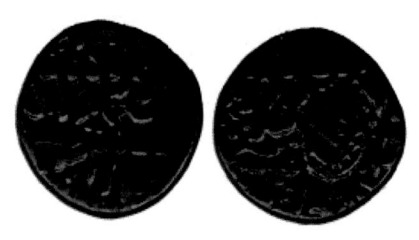

AD 1828/VS 1885
Authority: Ranjit Singh
Inscription: (as no. 3)

8.6g   21mm
1912,0709.430 Bleazby collection

300
Copper half paisa with a leaf on the reverse

AD 1828/VS 1885
Authority: Ranjit Singh
Inscription: (as no. 3)

8.5g   20mm
1912,0709.431 Bleazby collection

Catalogue Nos 301–311

301
Copper half paisa with a leaf on the reverse

AD 1828/VS 1885
Authority: Ranjit Singh
Inscription: (as no. 3)

8.6g   19mm
1912,0709.432 Bleazby collection

302
Copper half paisa with a leaf on the reverse

AD 1828/VS 1885
Authority: Ranjit Singh
Inscription: (as no. 3)

7.7g   20mm
1912,0709.433 Bleazby collection

303
Copper half paisa with a punch dagger on the obverse and a leaf on the reverse

AD 1828/VS 1885
Authority: Ranjit Singh
Inscription: (as no. 3)

8.0g   19mm
1912,0709.435 Bleazby collection

304
Copper half paisa with a leaf on the reverse

AD 1828/VS 1885
Authority: Ranjit Singh
Inscription: (as no. 3)

8.4g   19mm
1912,0709.439 Bleazby collection

305
Copper half paisa with a leaf on the reverse

AD 1828/VS 1885
Authority: Ranjit Singh
Inscription: (as no. 3)

8.9g   21mm
1912,0709.409 Bleazby collection

306
Copper half paisa with a leaf on the reverse

AD 1828/VS 1885
Authority: Ranjit Singh
Inscription: (as no. 3)

8.1g   20mm
1912,0709.414 Bleazby collection

307
Copper half paisa

AD 1834/VS 1891
Authority: Ranjit Singh

Obverse: Gurmukhi

ਸਮਤ ੧੮੯੧ਸਧਮ ਸੁਰ

Transliteration
Sambat 1891, sadam sur

Translation
Struck in the samvat year 1891

Reverse: as above

7.7g   21mm
OR 1723

308
Copper half paisa with a leaf on the reverse

AD 1828/VS 1885
Authority: Ranjit Singh
Inscription: (as no. 3)

9.4g   21mm
OR 1726

309
Copper half paisa with a leaf on the reverse

AD 1828/VS 1885
Authority: Ranjit Singh
Inscription: (as no. 3)

9.7g   21mm
OR 1727

310
Copper half paisa with a leaf on the reverse

AD 1828/VS 1885
Authority: Ranjit Singh
Inscription: (as no. 3)

8.5g   20mm
OR 1729

311
Copper half paisa with a leaf on the reverse

AD 1828/VS 1885
Authority: Ranjit Singh
Inscription: (as no. 3)

9.1g   21mm
1870,0507.13062 Freudenthal collection

312

Amritsar imitation copper coin with a leaf on the reverse

AD 1828/VS 1885
Authority: Ranjit Singh
Inscription: Illegible Gurmukhi inscription

5.2g 17mm
1860,1220.601 Major Hay collection

313

Copper half paisa with a leaf on the reverse

AD 1828/VS 1885
Authority: Ranjit Singh
Inscription: (as no. 3)

6.8g 20mm
1860,1220.602 Major Hay collection

314

Copper half paisa with a star symbol on the obverse and a leaf on the reverse

AD 1828/VS 1885
Authority: Ranjit Singh
Inscription: (as no. 3)

9.8g 23mm
1870,0507.13063 Freudenthal collection

315

Copper half paisa with a star symbol on the obverse and a leaf on the reverse

AD 1828/VS 1885
Authority: Ranjit Singh
Inscription: (as no. 3)
9.8g 19mm
1870,0507.13064 Freudenthal collection

316

Copper half paisa with a flag on the obverse and a leaf on the reverse

AD 1828/VS 1885
Authority: Ranjit Singh
Inscription: (as no. 3)

8.7g 19mm
OR 1731

317

Copper half paisa with a leaf on the reverse

AD 1828/VS 1885
Authority: Ranjit Singh
Inscription: (as no. 3)

11.3g 20mm
1885,0610.56 C.J. Rodgers collection

318

Copper half paisa with a leaf on the reverse

AD 1828/VS 1885
Authority: Ranjit Singh
Inscription: (as no. 291)

6.7g 20mm
1885,0610.58 C.J. Rodgers collection

319

Copper half paisa with a flower on the obverse and a leaf on the reverse

AD 1828/VS 1885
Authority: Ranjit Singh
Inscription: (as no. 3)

7.9g 19mm
1860,1220.603 Major Hay collection

320

Copper half paisa with a leaf on the reverse

AD 1828/VS 1885
Authority: Ranjit Singh
Inscription: (as no. 3)

9.0g 20mm
OR 1732

321

Copper fulus with a leaf on the reverse

AD 1844/VS 1901
Authority: Dulip Singh

Obverse: Gumukhi

ਬਾਬਾ ਨਾਨਕ ਜੀ ਸਹਾਇ

Transliteration
Baba Nanak Ji Sahai

Translation
Lord Nanak is the helper

Reverse: Persian

یک فلوس

Transliteration
Yek fulus

Translation
One fulus

7.8g 23mm
1912,0709.436 Bleazby collection

322

Copper fulus with a leaf on the reverse

AD 1828/VS 1885
Authority: Ranjit Singh
Inscription: (as no. 198)

6.8g 18mm
1885,0610.60 C.J. Rodgers collection

Catalogue Nos 323–333

323
Copper fulus with a leaf on the reverse

AD 1828/VS 1885
Authority: Ranjit Singh
Inscription: (as no. 198)

7.1g 18mm
1903,1009.56 Talbot collection

324
Copper fulus with a leaf on the reverse

AD 1828/VS 1885
Authority: Ranjit Singh
Inscription: (as no. 198)

6.9g 21mm
1920,0722.165 Dennehy collection

325
Copper fulus with a flower on the obverse and a leaf on the reverse

AD 1844/VS 1901
Authority: Dulip Singh
Inscription: (as no. 321)

9.9g 20mm
1903,1009.29 Talbot collection

326
Copper fulus with a flower on the obverse and a leaf on the reverse

AD 1844/VS 1901
Authority: Dulip Singh
Inscription: (as no. 321)

9.9g 21mm
1868,1236.89 Marsham collection

327
Copper fulus with flowers on the obverse and a leaf on the reverse

AD 1844/VS 1901
Authority: Dulip Singh
Inscription: (as no. 321)

10.0g 22mm
1903,1009.30 Talbot collection

328
Copper fulus with dot flowers on the obverse and a leaf on the reverse

AD 1844/VS 1901
Authority: Dulip Singh
Inscription: (as no. 321)

9.7g 22mm
1885,0610.62 C.J. Rodgers collection

329
Copper fulus with dot flowers on the obverse and a leaf on the reverse

AD 1843/VS 1900
Authority: Sher Singh
Inscription: (as no. 321)

9.9g 22mm
1889,1203.83 India Museum collection

330
Copper fulus with dot flowers on the obverse and a leaf on the reverse

AD 1843/VS 1900
Authority: Sher Singh
Inscription: (as no. 321)

9.8g 22mm
1885,0610.63 C.J. Rodgers collection

331
Copper fulus with dot flowers on the obverse and a leaf on the reverse

AD 1844/VS 1901
Authority: Dulip Singh
Inscription: (as no. 321)

9.9g 23mm
1903,1009.31 Talbot collection

332
Copper fulus with dot flowers on the obverse and a leaf on the reverse

AD 1844/VS 1901
Authority: Dulip Singh
Inscription: (as no. 321)

9.8g 22mm
1903,1009.28 Talbot collection

333
Copper quarter-anna

AD 1839/VS 1896
Authority: Ranjit Singh

Obverse: Persian

دیگ و تیغ و فتح نصرت بیدرنگ یافت از نانک گورو گوبند سنگ

Transliteration
Deg o tegh o fath nusrat bedrang Yaft az Nanak Guru Gobind Singh

Translation
Abundance, power and victory [and] assistance without delay are the gift of Nanak [and] Guru Gobind Singh

Reverse: Persian

پا انا نانک شای

Transliteration
Pa anna-i- Nanak shahi

Translation
¼ Anna of the Nanakshahi coin

8.0g 21mm
1903,1009.41 Talbot collection

Catalogue Nos 334–343

334
Copper quarter-anna with a leaf on the reverse

AD 1839/VS 1896
Authority: Ranjit Singh
Inscription: (as. no 333)

8.0g   19mm
OR 5049

335
Copper quarter-anna with a leaf on the reverse

AD 1839/VS 1896
Authority: Ranjit Singh
Inscription: (as. no 333)

6.8g   19mm
1885,0610.61 C.J. Rodgers collection

336
Copper quarter-anna with a leaf on the reverse

AD 1839/VS 1896
Authority: Ranjit Singh
Inscription: (as. no 333)

6.8g   19mm
1903,1009.43 Talbot collection

337
Copper quarter-anna with a leaf on the reverse

AD 1839/VS 1896
Authority: Ranjit Singh
Inscription: (as. no 333)

8.1g   20mm
OR 5050

Mint Anandgarh

To view referenced mint marks, see Appendix 2.

Silver coins

338
Silver rupee with a mint mark on the obverse and a flower on the reverse

AD 1784/VS 1841
Authority: Sikh Misal
Inscription: Gobindshahi couplet (as no. 15)

10.9g   21mm
1907,0702.23 Central Provinces of India collection

339
Silver rupee with a vsmall leaf on the reverse

AD 1786/VS 1843
Authority: Sikh Misal
Inscription: Gobindshahi couplet (as no. 15)

10.9g   22mm
1907,0702.22 Central Provinces of India collection

340
Silver rupee

AD 1787/VS 1844
Authority: Sikh Misal
Inscription: Gobindshahi couplet (as no. 15)
10.8g   22mm
1912,0709.315 Bleazby collection

341
Silver rupee

AD 1785/VS 1842
Authority: Sikh Misal
Inscription: Gobindshahi couplet (as no. 15)

10.7g   22mm
1912,0709.317 Bleazby collection

Mint Lahore

To view referenced mint marks, see Appendix 2.

Gold coins

342
Gold mohur with numerals 88 on the obverse and a leaf on the reverse

AD 1827/VS 1884
Authority: Ranjit Singh
Inscription: Nanakshahi couplet

Obverse: Persian

سکه زد بر سیم وزر فضل سچا صاحب است فتح
گوبند سنگه شا تیغ نانک واهب است

Transliteration
Sikka zad bar sim wa zar Fazl sacha sahib ast Fath Gobind Singh Shah Tegh Nanak wahib ast

Translation
The coin struck in silver and gold by the grace of the true Lord. Of the victory gained by the sword of Gobind Singh Shah Nanak is the provider

Reverse: Persian

ضرب دار السلطنت لاهور سنه جلوس میمنت مانوس

Transliteration
Zarb dar al-Sultanat Lahore Sanah Julus Maimanat Manus

Translation
Struck in the capital of Lahore during the prosperous human reign

10.8g   20mm
1912,0709.211 Bleazby collection

Silver coins

343
Silver rupee

AD 1765/VS 1822
Authority: Sikh Misal
Inscription: Gobindshahi couplet

Catalogue Nos 344–354

Obverse: Persian

دیگ تیغو فتح و نصرت بیدرنگ یافت از نانک گوروگوبند سنگه

Transliteration
Degh tegh o fath o nusrat bedrang Yaft az Nanak Guru Gobind Singh

Translation
Abundance, power and victory [and assistance without delay are the gift of Nanak [and] Guru Gobind Singh

Reverse: Persian

ضرب دار السلطنت لاهور سنه جلوس میمنت مانوس

Transliteration
Zarb dar al-Sultanat Lahore Sanah Julus Maimanat Manus

Translation
Struck in the capital of Lahore during the prosperous human reign

11.2g 22mm
1936,1017.2 Baldwin collection

344
Silver rupee

AD 1766/VS 1823
Authority: Sikh Misal
Inscription: Gobindshahi couplet (as.no 343)

11.3g 21mm
1912,0709.319 Bleazby collection

345
Silver rupee

AD 1767/VS 1824
Authority: Sikh Misal
Inscription: Gobindshahi couplet (as.no 343)

11.1g 20mm
1912,0709.318 Bleazby collection

346
Silver rupee

AD 1768/VS 1825
Authority: Sikh Misal
Inscription: Gobindshahi couplet (as.no 343)

10.7g 21mm
1912,0709.331 Bleazby collection

347
Silver rupee

AD 1769/VS 1826
Authority: Sikh Misal
Inscription: Gobindshahi couplet (as.no 343)

11.2g 22mm
1912,0709.320 Bleazby collection

348
Silver rupee

AD 1770/VS 1827
Authority: Sikh Misal
Inscription: Gobindshahi couplet (as.no 343)

11.4g 21mm
1912,0709.321 Bleazby collection

349
Silver rupee

AD 1771/VS 1828
Authority: Sikh Misal
Inscription: Gobindshahi couplet (as.no 343)

11.3g 21mm
1912,0709.322 Bleazby collection

350
Silver rupee

AD 1772/VS 1829
Authority: Sikh Misal
Inscription: Gobindshahi couplet (as.no 343)

11.2g 21mm
1912,0709.323 Bleazby collection

351
Silver rupee

AD 1773/VS 1830
Authority: Sikh Misal
Inscription: Gobindshahi couplet (as.no 343)

11.2g 21mm
1912,0709.324 Bleazby collection

352
Silver rupee

AD 1774/VS 1831
Authority: Sikh Misal
Inscription: Gobindshahi couplet (as.no 343)

10.9g 22mm
1912,0709.325 Bleazby collection

353
Silver rupee

AD 1775/VS 1832
Authority: Sikh Misal
Inscription: Gobindshahi couplet (as.no 343)

11.2g 22mm
1912,0709.326 Bleazby collection

354
Silver rupee

AD 1776/VS 1833
Authority: Sikh Misal
Inscription: Gobindshahi couplet (as.no 343)

11.1g 21mm
1912,0709.328 Bleazby collection

355

Silver rupee

AD 1777/VS 1834
Authority: Sikh Misal
Inscription: Gobindshahi couplet (as.no 343)

11.1g   20mm
1912,0709.329 Bleazby collection

356

Silver rupee

AD 1778/VS 1835
Authority: Sikh Misal
Inscription: Gobindshahi couplet (as.no 343)

11.1g   20mm
1912,0709.330 Bleazby collection

357

Silver rupee

AD 1779/VS 1836
Authority: Sikh Misal
Inscription: Gobindshahi couplet (as.no 343)

11.2g   21mm
1889,1203.91 India Museum collection

358

Silver rupee

AD 1783/VS 1840
Authority: Sikh Misal
Inscription: Gobindshahi couplet (as.no 343)

11.1g   20mm
1912,0709.332 Bleazby collection

359

Silver rupee

AD 1784/VS 1841
Authority: Sikh Misal
Inscription: Nanakshahi couplet (as no. 342)

11.1g   24mm
1936,1017.3 Baldwin collection

360

Silver rupee

AD 1785/VS 1842
Authority: Sikh Misal
Inscription: Nanakshahi couplet (as no. 342)

11.0g   23mm
1936,1017.15 Baldwin collection

361

Silver rupee

AD 1787/VS 1844
Authority: Sikh Misal
Inscription: Nanakshahi couplet (as no. 342)

11.0g   23mm
1936,1017.5 Baldwin collection

362

Silver rupee with a plant on the reverse

AD 1792/VS 1849
Authority: Sikh Misal
Inscription: Nanakshahi couplet (as no. 342)

10.9g   24mm
1912,0709.333 Bleazby collection

363

Silver rupee with a plant on the reverse

AD 1793/VS 1850
Authority: Sikh Misal
Inscription: Nanakshahi couplet (as no. 342)

10.3g   23mm
1912,0709.334 Bleazby collection

364

Silver rupee

AD 1794/VS 1851
Authority: Sikh Misal
Inscription: Nanakshahi couplet (as no. 342)

10.7g   23mm
1912,0709.335 Bleazby collection

365

Silver rupee

AD 1795/VS 1852
Authority: Sikh Misal
Inscription: Nanakshahi couplet (as no. 342)
10.4g   24mm
1912,0709.336 Bleazby collection

366

Silver rupee

AD 1796/VS 1853
Authority: Sikh Misal
Inscription: Nanakshahi couplet (as no. 342)

10.7g   23mm
1912,0709.337 Bleazby collection

Catalogue Nos 367–378

367
Silver rupee with a leaf on the reverse

AD 1799/VS 1856
Authority: Sikh Misal
Inscription: Nanakshahi couplet (as no. 342)

11.1g   23mm
1936,1017.50 Baldwin collection

368
Silver rupee with a leaf on the reverse

AD 1800/VS 1857
Authority: Sikh Misal
Inscription: Nanakshahi couplet (as no. 342)

11.1g   24mm
1912,0709.233 Bleazby collection

369
Silver half rupee

AD 1775/VS 1832
Authority: Sikh Misal
Inscription: Gobindshahi couplet (as no. 343)

5.5g   20mm
1936,1017.51 Baldwin collection

370
Silver rupee with a leaf on the reverse

AD 1801/VS 1858
Authority: Ranjit Singh
Inscription: Nanakshahi couplet (as no. 342)

11.1g   25mm
1912,0709.234 Bleazby collection

371
Silver rupee with a leaf on the reverse

AD 1802/VS 1859
Authority: Ranjit Singh
Inscription: Nanakshahi couplet (as no. 342)

11.1g   24mm
1936,1017.21 Baldwin collection

372
Silver rupee with a leaf on the reverse

AD 1804/VS 1861
Authority: Ranjit Singh
Inscription: Nanakshahi couplet (as no. 342)

11.0g   24mm
1920,1002.8 Mavrogordato collection

373
Silver rupee with a leaf on the reverse

AD 1805/VS 1862
Authority: Ranjit Singh
Inscription: Nanakshahi couplet (as no. 342)

11.1g   24mm
1912,0709.235 Bleazby collection

374
Silver rupee with a leaf on the reverse

AD 1806/VS 1863
Authority: Ranjit Singh
Inscription: Nanakshahi couplet (as no. 342)

11.1g   23mm
1912,0709.236 Bleazby collection

375
Silver rupee with a leaf on the reverse

AD 1810/VS 1867
Authority: Ranjit Singh
Inscription: Nanakshahi couplet (as no. 342)

11.0g   22mm
1936,1017.9 Baldwin collection

376
Silver rupee with a leaf on the reverse

AD 1811/VS 1868
Authority: Ranjit Singh
Inscription: Nanakshahi couplet (as no. 342)

11.0g   22mm
1936,1017.41 Baldwin collection

377
Silver rupee with a leaf on the reverse

AD 1812/VS 1869
Authority: Ranjit Singh
Inscription: Nanakshahi couplet (as no. 342)

11.0g   22mm
1912,0709.237 Bleazby collection

378
Silver rupee with a leaf on the reverse

AD 1814/VS 1871
Authority: Ranjit Singh
Inscription: Nanakshahi couplet (as no. 342)

11.0g   22mm
1912,0709.238 Bleazby collection

379
Silver rupee with a leaf on the reverse

AD 1815/VS 1872
Authority: Ranjit Singh
Inscription: Nanakshahi couplet (as no. 342)

11.0g 23mm
1936,1017.6 Baldwin collection

380
Silver rupee with a leaf on the reverse

AD 1816/VS 1873
Authority: Ranjit Singh
Inscription: Nanakshahi couplet (as no. 342)

11.1g 21mm
1912,0709.239 Bleazby collection

381
Silver rupee with a leaf on the reverse

AD 1817/VS 1874
Authority: Ranjit Singh
Inscription: Nanakshahi couplet (as no. 342)

11.1g 22mm
1936,1017.16 Baldwin collection

382
Silver rupee with a leaf on the reverse

AD 1820/VS 1877
Authority: Ranjit Singh
Inscription: Nanakshahi couplet (as no. 342)

11.0g 22mm
1936,1017.40 Baldwin collection

383
Silver rupee with a leaf on the reverse

AD 1822/VS 1879
Authority: Ranjit Singh
Inscription: Nanakshahi couplet (as no. 342)

11.1g 23mm
1912,0709.240 Bleazby collection

384
Silver rupee with a leaf on the reverse

AD 1824/VS 1881
Authority: Ranjit Singh
Inscription: Nanakshahi couplet (as no. 342)

11.1g 24mm
1936,1017.32 Baldwin collection

385
Silver rupee with a leaf and a star on the reverse

AD 1825/VS 1882
Authority: Ranjit Singh
Inscription: Nanakshahi couplet (as no. 342)

11.1g 23mm
1912,0709.246 Bleazby collection

386
Silver rupee with a leaf and a star on the reverse

AD 1826/VS 1883
Authority: Ranjit Singh
Inscription: Nanakshahi couplet (as no. 342)

11.1g 23mm
1912,0709.247 Bleazby collection

387
Silver rupee with the numerals 88 on the obverse and a leaf on the reverse

AD 1827/VS 1884
Authority: Ranjit Singh
Inscription: Nanakshahi couplet (as no. 342)

11.1g 23mm
1912,0709.244 Bleazby collection

388
Silver rupee with the numerals 88 on the obverse and a leaf on the reverse

AD 1827/VS 1884
Authority: Ranjit Singh
Inscription: Nanakshahi couplet (as no. 342)

11.0g 23mm
1912,0709.243 Bleazby collection

389
Silver rupee with the numerals 87 on the obverse and a leaf on the reverse

AD 1827/VS 1884
Authority: Ranjit Singh
Inscription: Nanakshahi couplet (as no. 342)

11.0g 23mm
1912,0709.242 Bleazby collection

390
Silver rupee with the numerals 90 on the obverse and a leaf on the reverse

AD 1827/VS 1884
Authority: Ranjit Singh
Inscription: Nanakshahi couplet (as no. 342)

11.1g 23mm
1912,0709.245 Bleazby collection

Catalogue Nos 391–402

391
Silver rupee with the numerals 88 on the obverse and a leaf on the reverse

AD 1827/VS 1884
Authority: Ranjit Singh
Inscription: Nanakshahi couplet (as no. 342)

11.1g   22mm
1887,0508.8 Theobald collection

392
Silver rupee with dot flowers on the obverse and a leaf on the reverse

AD 1828/VS 1885
Authority: Ranjit Singh
Inscription: Nanakshahi couplet (as no. 342)

11.1g   22mm
1912,0709.241 Bleazby collection

393
Silver rupee with dot flowers on the obverse and a leaf on the reverse

AD 1828/VS 1885
Authority: Ranjit Singh
Inscription: Nanakshahi couplet (as no. 342)

11.1g   23mm
1887,0508.6 Theobald collection

394
Silver rupee with numerals 96 on the obverse and a leaf on the reverse

AD 1828/VS 1885
Authority: Ranjit Singh
Inscription: Nanakshahi couplet (as no. 342)

11.1g   23mm
1936,1017.54 Baldwin collection

395
Silver rupee with numerals 96 on the obverse and a leaf on the reverse

AD 1828/VS 1885
Authority: Ranjit Singh
Inscription: Nanakshahi couplet (as no. 342)

11.1g   24mm
1931,0809.3 Ingliss collection

396
Copper paisa with a leaf on the reverse

AD 1824/VS 1881
Authority: Ranjit Singh
Inscription: Gobindshahi couplet (as no. 343)

11.3g   21mm
1885,0610.48 C.J. Rodgers collection

397
Copper paisa with a leaf on the reverse

AD 1823/VS 1880
Authority: Ranjit Singh
Inscription: Gobindshahi couplet (as no. 343)

11.6g   21mm
1909,1007.4 Sutcliffe collection

398
Copper paisa with a leaf on the reverse

AD 1823/VS 1880
Authority: Ranjit Singh
Inscription: Gobindshahi couplet (as no. 343)

11.7g   23mm
1903,1009.62 Talbot collection

399
Copper paisa

AD 1823/VS 1880
Authority: Ranjit Singh
Inscription: Gobindshahi couplet (as no. 343)

11.8g   26mm
1903,1009.65 Talbot collection

400
Copper paisa with a leaf on the reverse

AD 1824/VS 1881
Authority: Ranjit Singh
Inscription: Gobindshahi couplet (as no. 343)

11.7g   23mm
1912,0709.356 Bleazby collection

401
Copper paisa with a leaf on the reverse

AD 1823/VS 1880
Authority: Ranjit Singh
Inscription: Gobindshahi couplet (as no. 343)

11.7g   23mm
1885,0610.46 C.J. Rodgers collection

Mint Multan

To view referenced mint marks, see Appendix 2.

Silver coins

402
Silver rupee

AD 1772/VS 1829

56 | Catalogue of Sikh Coins in the British Museum

Authority: Sikh Misal
Inscription: Gobindshahi couplet

Obverse: Persian

دیگ و تیغ و فتح نصرت بیدرنگ یافت از نانک گوروگوبند سنگ

Transliteration
Deg o tegh o fath nusrat bedrang Yaft az Nanak Guru Gobind Singh

Translation
Abundance, power and victory [and] assistance without delay are the gift of Nanak [and] Guru Gobind Singh

Reverse: Persian

ضرب دار الامان ملتان سمبت جلوس میمنت مانوس

Transliteration
Zarb Dar Al-Aman Multan Sambat Julus Maimanat Manus

Translation
Struck in Multan, the abode of safety in the year of the prosperous reign

11.4g   21mm
1922,0424.2361 Whitehead collection

403
Silver rupee with a small flower on the reverse

AD 1773/VS 1830
Authority: Sikh Misal
Inscription: Gobindshahi couplet (as no. 402)

11.4g   21mm
1922,0424.2362 Whitehead collection

404
Silver rupee with a small flower on the reverse

AD 1774/VS 1831
Authority: Sikh Misal
Inscription: Gobindshahi couplet (as no. 402)

11.5g   21mm
1922,0424.2363 Whitehead collection

405
Silver rupee with a small flower on the reverse

AD 1775/VS 1832
Authority: Sikh Misal
Inscription: Gobindshahi couplet (as no. 402)

11.5g   20mm
1922,0424.2365 Whitehead collection

406
Silver rupee

AD 1776/VS 1833
Authority: Sikh Misal
Inscription: Gobindshahi couplet (as no. 402)

11.5g   22mm
1922,0424.2366 Whitehead collection

407
Silver rupee with a small flower on the reverse

AD 1775/VS 1832
Authority: Sikh Misal
Inscription: Gobindshahi couplet (as no. 402)

11.5g   20mm
1936,1017.34 Baldwin collection

408
Silver rupee with a small flower on the reverse

AD 1777/VS 1834
Authority: Sikh Misal
Inscription: Gobindshahi couplet (as no. 402)

11.5g   21mm
1922,0424.2367 Whitehead collection

409
Silver rupee with a small flower on the reverse

AD 1778/VS 1835
Authority: Sikh Misal
Inscription: Gobindshahi couplet (as no. 402)

11.5g   21mm
1922,0424.2368 Whitehead collection

410
Silver rupee with a mint mark on the reverse

AD 1779/VS 1836
Authority: Sikh Misal
Inscription: Gobindshahi couplet (as no. 402)

11.4g   21mm
1922,0424.2369 Whitehead collection

411
Silver rupee with a leaf on the reverse

AD 1818/VS 1875
Authority: Ranjit Singh
Inscription: Nanakshahi couplet

Obverse: Persian

سکه زد بر سیم وزر فضل سچا صاحب است فتح گوبند سنگه شا تیغ نانک واهب است

Transliteration
Sikka zad bar sim wa zar Fazl sacha sahib ast Fath Gobind Singh Shah Tegh Nanak wahib ast

Translation
The coin struck in silver and gold by the grace of the true Lord. Of the victory gained by the sword of Gobind Singh Shah Nanak is the provider

Reverse: Persian

ضرب دار الامان ملتان سمبت جلوس میمنت مانوس

Transliteration
Zarb Dar Al-Aman Multan Sambat Julus Maimanat Manus

Translation
Struck in Multan, the abode of safety in the year of the prosperous reign

10.9g 23mm
1912,0709.212 Bleazby collection

412
Silver rupee with a leaf on the reverse

AD 1819/VS 1876
Authority: Ranjit Singh
Inscription: Nanakshahi couplet (as no. 411)

11.0g 23mm
1936,1017.35 Baldwin collection

413
Silver rupee with a leaf on the reverse

AD 1820/VS 1877
Authority: Ranjit Singh
Inscription: Nanakshahi couplet (as no. 411)
11.1g 24mm
1912,0709.267 Bleazby collection

414
Silver rupee with a leaf on the reverse

AD 1822/VS 1879
Authority: Ranjit Singh
Inscription: Nanakshahi couplet (as no. 411)

11.0g 23mm
1922,0424.2839 Whitehead collection

415
Silver rupee with a trident on the obverse and a leaf on the reverse

AD 1823/VS 1880
Authority: Ranjit Singh
Inscription: Nanakshahi couplet (as no. 411)

11.0g 23mm
1936,1017.59 Baldwin collection

416
Silver rupee with a trident on the obverse and a leaf on the reverse

AD 1824/VS 1881
Authority: Ranjit Singh
Inscription: Nanakshahi couplet (as no. 411)

11.1g 24mm
1936,1017.14 Baldwin collection

417
Silver rupee with a trident on the obverse and a leaf and small flower on the reverse

AD 1825/VS 1882
Authority: Ranjit Singh
Inscription: Nanakshahi couplet (as no. 411)

11.1g 23mm
1936,1017.56 Baldwin collection

418
Silver rupee with a trident on the obverse and a leaf on the reverse

AD 1827/VS 1884
Authority: Ranjit Singh
Inscription: Nanakshahi couplet (as no. 411)

11.1g 23mm
1936,1017.58 Baldwin collection

419
Silver rupee with a flower on the obverse and a leaf on the reverse

AD 1835/VS 1892
Authority: Ranjit Singh
Inscription: Nanakshahi couplet (as no. 411)

11.1g 22mm
1922,0424.2840 Whitehead collection

420
Silver rupee with a flower on the obverse and a leaf on the reverse

AD 1828/VS 1885
Authority: Ranjit Singh
Inscription: Nanakshahi couplet (as no. 411)

11.1g 22mm
1936,1017.57 Baldwin collection

421
Silver rupee with a flower on the obverse and a leaf on the reverse

AD 1829/VS 1886
Authority: Ranjit Singh
Inscription: Nanakshahi couplet (as no. 411)

11.1g 23mm
1912,0709.213 Bleazby collection

422
Silver rupee with a leaf on the reverse

AD 1830/VS 1887
Authority: Ranjit Singh
Inscription: Nanakshahi couplet (as no. 411)

11.1g 22mm
1887,0508.9 Theobald collection

423
Silver rupee a leaf on the reverse

AD 1831/VS 1888
Authority: Ranjit Singh
Inscription: Nanakshahi couplet (as no. 411)

11.1g 23mm
1912,0709.308 Bleazby collection

424

Silver rupee a leaf on the reverse

AD 1832/VS 1889
Authority: Ranjit Singh
Inscription: Nanakshahi couplet (as no. 411)

11.1g 22mm
1912,0709.316 Bleazby collection

425

Silver rupee a leaf on the reverse

AD 1832/VS 1889
Authority: Ranjit Singh
Inscription: Nanakshahi couplet (as no. 411)

11.1g 22mm
1912,0709.214 Bleazby collection

426

Silver rupee with a mint mark on the obverse and a leaf on the reverse

AD 1833/VS 1890
Authority: Ranjit Singh
Inscription: Nanakshahi couplet (as no. 411)

11.1g 23mm
1912,0709.215 Bleazby collection

427

Silver rupee with a mint mark on the obverse and a leaf on the reverse

AD 1834/VS 1891
Authority: Ranjit Singh
Inscription: Nanakshahi couplet (as no. 411)

11.0g 21mm
1912,0709.216 Bleazby collection

428

Silver rupee with a mint mark on the obverse and a leaf on the reverse

AD 1835/VS 1892
Authority: Ranjit Singh
Inscription: Nanakshahi couplet (as no. 411)

11.1g 22mm
1922,0424.2364 Whitehead collection

429

Silver rupee with a mint mark on the obverse and a leaf on the reverse

AD 1837/VS 1894
Authority: Ranjit Singh
Inscription: Nanakshahi couplet (as no. 411)

11.1g 21mm
1912,0709.253 Bleazby collection

430

Silver rupee with a mint mark on the obverse and a leaf on the reverse

AD 1838/VS 1895
Authority: Ranjit Singh
Inscription: Nanakshahi couplet (as no. 411)

11.1g 24mm
1936,1017.8 Baldwin collection

431

Silver rupee with a mint mark on the obverse and a leaf on the reverse

AD 1839/VS 1896
Authority: Ranjit Singh
Inscription: Nanakshahi couplet (as no. 411)

11.1g 24mm
1912,0709.249 Bleazby collection

432

Silver rupee with a mint mark on the obverse and a leaf on the reverse

AD 1840/VS 1897
Authority: Kharak Singh
Inscription: Nanakshahi couplet (as no. 411)

11.1g 23mm
1912,0709.217 Bleazby collection

433

Silver rupee with a mint mark on the obverse and a leaf on the reverse

AD 1840/VS 1897
Authority: Kharak Singh
Inscription: Nanakshahi couplet (as no. 411)

11.1g 22mm
1922,0424.2371 Whitehead collection

434

Silver rupee with a leaf on the reverse

AD 1841/VS 1898
Authority: Kharak Singh
Inscription: Nanakshahi couplet (as no. 411)

11.1g 24mm
1912,0709.218 Bleazby collection

435

Silver rupee with a leaf on the reverse

AD 1842/VS 1899
Authority: Sher Singh
Inscription: Nanakshahi couplet (as no. 411)

11.1g 22mm
1912,0709.257 Bleazby collection

Catalogue Nos 436–444

436
Silver rupee with a leaf on the reverse

AD 1843/VS 1900
Authority: Sher Singh
Inscription: Nanakshahi couplet (as no. 411)

11.1g 24mm
1922,0424.2370 Whitehead collection

437
Silver rupee with a leaf on the reverse

AD 1844/VS 1901
Authority: Dulip Singh
Inscription: Nanakshahi couplet (as no. 411)

11.1g 25mm
1922,0424.2838 Whitehead collection

438
Silver rupee with a leaf on the reverse

AD 1847/VS 1904
Authority: Dulip Singh
Inscription: Nanakshahi couplet (as no. 411)

11.1g 23mm
1912,0709.219 Bleazby collection

Copper coins

439
Copper paisa with a flower on the obverse and a leaf on the reverse

AD 1777/VS 1834
Authority: Sikh Misal

Obverse: Persian

ضرب ملتان خلوس مبارک

Transliteration
Zarb Multan julus Mubarak

Translation
Struck in Multan during the auspicious reign

Reverse: Persian

فلوس گورو گوبند سنگه جیو

Transliteration
Fulus Guru Gobind Singh Jiyo

Translation
Copper fulus of Guru Gobind Singh

11.7g 22mm
1885,0610.45 C.J. Rodgers collection

440
Copper paisa with a flower on the obverse and a leaf on the reverse

AD 1825/VS 1882
Authority: Ranjit Singh
Inscription: Nanakshahi couplet

Obverse: Persian

سکه زد بر سیم وزر فصل سچا صاحب است فتح
گوبند سنگه شاهن تیغ نانک واهب است

Transliteration
Sikka zad bar sim wa zar Fazl sacha sahib ast Fath Gobind Singh Shahan Tegh Nanak wahib ast

Translation
The coin struck in silver and gold by the grace of the true Lord. Of the victory gained by the sword of Gobind Singh, King of Kings, Nanak is the provider

Reverse: Persian

ضرب جلوس ملتان

Transliteration
Zarb julus Multan

Translation
Struck in the year in Multan

12.5g 23mm
1912,0709.369 Bleazby collection

441
Copper paisa with a flower on the obverse and a leaf on the reverse

AD 1825/VS 1882
Authority: Ranjit Singh
Inscription: Nanakshahi couplet (as no. 440)

12.2g 23mm
1903,1009.94 Talbot collection

442
Copper paisa with a flower on the obverse and a leaf on the reverse

AD 1847/VS 1904
Authority: Ranjit Singh
Inscription: Nanakshahi couplet (as no. 440)

11.8g 25mm
1860,1220.577 Major Hay collection

Small gold coins

443
One-twentieth of a gold mohur with a leaf on the reverse

AD 1848/VS 1905
Authority: Governor Diwan Mulraj

Obverse: Persian

سهای ستگورو

Transliteration
Sahai satguru

Translation
May the true teacher help

Reverse: Persian

مندرکا

Transliteration
Mundarka

Translation
Siege

0.6g 9mm
OR 5961

444
One-twentieth of a gold mohur with small crosses on the obverse and a leaf on the reverse

AD 1848/VS 1905
Authority: Governor Diwan Mulraj

Inscription: (same as no. 443)

0.6g 8mm
1934,0303.19 Clark collection

445

One-twentieth of a gold mohur with small crosses on the obverse and a leaf on the reverse

AD 1848/VS 1905
Authority: Governor Diwan Mulraj
Inscription: (same as no. 443)

0.6g 9mm
1912,0709.339 Bleazby collection

446

One-twentieth of a gold mohur with a mint mark on the obverse and a leaf on the reverse

AD 1848/VS 1905
Authority: Governor Diwan Mulraj
Inscription: (same as no. 443)

0.6g 8mm
1870,0302.4 Cutter collection

447

One-twentieth of a gold mohur with a leaf on the reverse

AD 1848/VS 1905
Authority: Governor Diwan Mulraj
Inscription: (same as no. 443)

0.6g 9mm
1860,1220.533 Hay collection

448

One-twentieth of a gold mohur with a leaf on the reverse

AD 1848/VS 1905

Authority: Governor Diwan Mulraj
Inscription: (same as no. 443)

0.6g 9mm
1874,1001.7 Gutherie collection

449

One-twentieth of a gold mohur with a leaf on the reverse

AD 1848/VS 1905
Authority: Governor Diwan Mulraj
Inscription: (same as no. 443)

0.6g 9mm
1875,0502.137 Lincoln collection

450

One-twentieth of a gold mohur with a leaf on the reverse

AD 1848/VS 1905
Authority: Governor Diwan Mulraj
Inscription: (same as no. 443)

0.6g 8mm
1920,0813.663 Frampton collection

451

One-twentieth of a gold mohur with a leaf on the reverse

AD 1848/VS 1905
Authority: Governor Diwan Mulraj
Inscription: (same as no. 443)

0.6g 10mm
1870,0302.3 Cutter collection

452

One-twentieth of a gold mohur with a leaf on the reverse

AD 1848/VS 1905

Authority: Governor Diwan Mulraj
Inscription: (same as no. 443)

0.6g 9mm
1870,0302.2 Cutter collection

453

One-twentieth of a gold mohur with a mint mark on the obverse and a leaf on the reverse

AD 1848/VS 1905
Authority: Governor Diwan Mulraj
Inscription: (same as no. 443)

0.6g 9mm
1875,0502.138 Lincoln collection

454

One-twentieth of a gold mohur with a mint mark on the obverse and a leaf on the reverse

AD 1848/VS 1905
Authority: Governor Diwan Mulraj
Inscription: (same as no. 443)

0.6g 9mm
1850,1120.1 Carmichael Smyth collection

456

One-twentieth of a gold mohur with a mint mark on the obverse and a leaf on the reverse

AD 1848/VS 1905
Authority: Governor Diwan Mulraj
Inscription: (same as no. 443)

0.6g 9mm
1874,1001.8 Gutherie collection

456

One-twentieth of a gold mohur with a leaf on the reverse

AD 1848/VS 1905

Catalogue Nos 457–464

Authority: Governor Diwan Mulraj
Inscription: (same as no. 443)

0.6g 9mm
IOC.2167 India Office Collection

457

One-twentieth of a gold mohur with a leaf on the reverse

AD 1848/VS 1905
Authority: Governor Diwan Mulraj
Inscription: (same as no. 443)

0.6g 9mm
1870,0302.5 Cutter Collection

Mint Peshawar

To view referenced mint marks, see Appendix 2.

Silver coins

458

Silver rupee with a leaf on the obverse and dots on the reverse

AD 1835/VS 1892
Authority: Governor Hari Singh Nalwa
Inscription: Gobindshahi couplet

Obverse: Persian

دیگ تیغ فتح نصرت بیدرنگ یافت از نانک گورگوبند سنگ

Transliteration
Deg tegh fath nusrat bedrang Yaft az Nanak Gur Gobind Singh

Translation
Abundance, power and victory [and] assistance without delay are the gift of Nanak [and] Guru Gobind Singh

Reverse: Persian

ضرب پشاور جلوس سنه

Transliteration
Zarb Peshawar Julus Sanah

Translation
Struck in Peshawar in the prosperous year

8.4g 24mm
1936,1017.11 Baldwin Collection

459

Silver rupee with a small star in centre on the obverse and a leaf with dots and numerals 189 on the reverse

AD 1836/VS 1893
Authority: Governor Hari Singh Nalwa
Inscription: Gobindshahi couplet (as no. 458)

8.4g 24mm
1850,0305.657 Edward Thomas Collection

460

Silver rupee with a small star in centre on the obverse and a leaf with dots and numerals 189 on the reverse

AD 1836/VS 1893
Authority: Governor Hari Singh Nalwa
Inscription: Gobindshahi couplet (as no. 458)

8.4g 24mm
1912,0709.220 Bleazby Collection

461

Silver rupee with a milled edge, small star in centre on the obverse and a leaf with dots and numerals 189 on the reverse

AD 1837/VS 1894
Authority: Governor Hari Singh Nalwa
Inscription: Gobindshahi couplet (as no. 458)

11.1g 26mm
1912,0709.221 Bleazby Collection

462

Silver rupee with a small star in centre on the obverse and a leaf with dots and numerals 189 on the reverse

AD 1837/VS 1894
Authority: Governor Hari Singh Nalwa
Inscription: Gobindshahi couplet (as no. 458)

8.4g 24mm
1889,1203.168 India Museum Collection

Copper coins

463

Copper paisa with a small star in centre on the obverse and a leaf with dots and numerals 189 on the reverse

AD 1837/VS 1894
Authority: Ranjit Singh
Inscription: Gobindshahi couplet (as no. 458)

7.4g 24mm
1912,0709.362 Bleazby Collection

464

Copper paisa with a peacock on the obverse

AD 1834/VS 1891
Authority: Ranjit Singh
Inscription

Obverse: Persian

پشاور

Transliteration
Peshawar

Translation
Peshawar

Reverse: Gurmukhi

Illegible Gurmukhi inscription

7.7g 19mm
1935,1109.47 Horwood Collection

Mint Kashmir

To view referenced mint marks, see Appendix 2.

Silver coins

465

Silver rupee with a small plant on the obverse and a leaf on the reverse

AD 1819/VS 1876
Authority: Ranjit Singh
Inscription: Gobindshahi couplet

Obverse: Persian

دیگ و تیغ و فتح و نصرت بیدرنگ یافت از نانک گورو گوبند سنگ

Transliteration
Deg o tegh o fath o nusrat bedrang Yaft az Nanak Guru Gobind Singh

Translation
Abundance, power and victory [and] assistance without delay are the gift of Nanak [and] Guru Gobind Singh

Reverse: Persian

ضرب سمبت کشمیر خطہ

Transliteration
Zarb Sambat Kashmir Khitta

Translation
Struck in the Sambat year in the Kashmir district

10.9g   22mm
1912,0709.223 Bleazby Collection

466

Silver rupee with a small plant on the obverse and a leaf on the reverse

AD 1819/VS 1876
Authority: Ranjit Singh
Inscription: Gobindshahi couplet (as no. 465)

10.8g   21mm
1912,0709.224 Bleazby Collection

467

Silver rupee with a small plant on the obverse and a leaf on the reverse

AD 1819/VS 1876
Authority: Ranjit Singh
Inscription: Gobindshahi couplet (as no. 465)

10.9g   22mm
1909,0207.9 Gaskill Collection

468

Silver rupee with a small plant on the obverse and a leaf on the reverse

AD 1820/VS 1877
Authority: Ranjit Singh
Inscription: Gobindshahi couplet

Obverse: Persian

دیگ و تیغ و فتح و نصرت بیدرنگ یافت از نانک گورو گوبند سنگ

Transliteration
Deg o tegh o fath o nusrat bedrang Yaft az Nanak Guru Gobind Singh

Translation
Abundance, power and victory [and] assistance without delay are the gift of Nanak [and] Guru Gobind Singh

Reverse: Persian

ضرب سمبت خطہ کشمیر جلوس میمنت مانوس

Transliteration
Zarb Sambat Khitta Kashmir Julus Maimanat Manus

Translation
Struck in the Sambat year in the prosperous reign in the Kashmir district

11.0g   22mm
1912,0709.225 Bleazby Collection

469

Silver rupee with a leaf on the reverse

AD 1821/VS 1878
Authority: Ranjit Singh

Inscription: Gobindshahi couplet (as no. 468)
With the Gurmukhi word ਹਰ (har) meaning 'almighty' on the obverse

11.0g   23mm
1912,0709.226 Bleazby Collection

470

Silver rupee with a leaf on the reverse

AD 1822/VS 1879
Authority: Ranjit Singh
Inscription: Gobindshahi couplet (as no. 468)
With the Nagri word हर (har) meaning 'almighty' on the obverse

10.9g   22mm
1936,1017.36 Baldwin Collection

471

Silver rupee with a leaf on the reverse

AD 1822/VS 1879
Authority: Ranjit Singh
Inscription: Gobindshahi couplet (as no. 468)
With the Nagri word ओम (om), celestial sound on the obverse

11.0g   21mm
1936,1017.37 Baldwin Collection

472

Silver rupee with a mint mark on the obverse and a leaf on the reverse

AD 1827/VS 1884
Authority: Ranjit Singh
Inscription: Gobindshahi couplet

Obverse: Persian

دیگ و تیغ و فتح و نصرت بیدرنگ یافت از نانک گورو گوبند سنگ

Transliteration
Deg o tegh o fath o nusrat bedrang Yaft az Nanak Guru Gobind Singh

Translation
Abundance, power and victory [and] assistance without delay are the gift of Nanak [and] Guru Gobind Singh

Catalogue Nos 473–481

Reverse: Persian

سمبت اکال سهای خطه کشمیر ضرب

Transliteration
Sambat Akal Sahai Khitta Kashmir Zarb

Translation
Struck in the Sambat year with the help of the immortal Lord

11.0g 21mm
1903,1009.10 Talbot Collection

473
Silver rupee with a mint mark on the obverse and a leaf on the reverse

AD 1827/VS 1884
Authority: Ranjit Singh
Inscription: Gobindshahi couplet (as no. 472)

10.9g 21mm
1903,1009.5 Talbot Collection

474
Silver rupee with a mint mark on the obverse and a leaf on the reverse

AD 1828/VS 1885
Authority: Ranjit Singh
Inscription: Gobindshahi couplet

Obverse: Persian

دیگ و تیغ و فتح و نصرت بیدرنگ یافت از نانک گورو گوبند سنگ

Transliteration
Deg o tegh o fath o nusrat bedrang Yaft az Nanak Guru Gobind Singh

Translation
Abundance, power and victory [and] assistance without delay are the gift of Nanak [and] Guru Gobind Singh

Reverse: Persian

سنه ضرب بخت اکال تخت جلوس میمنت مانوس کشمیر

Transliteration
Sanah Zarb bakht Akal Takht Julus Maimanat Manus Kashmir

Translation
Struck in the city of Kashmir under the fortunate rule of the Takht Akal during the prosperous human reign

11.0g 21mm
1936,1017.52 Baldwin Collection

475
Silver rupee with a plant on the obverse and a leaf on the reverse

AD 1830/VS 1887
Authority: Ranjit Singh
Inscription: Gobindshahi couplet (as no. 474)

11.0g 21mm
OR 5042

476
Silver rupee with a plant on the obverse and a leaf on the reverse

AD 1830/VS 1887
Authority: Ranjit Singh
Inscription: Gobindshahi couplet (as no. 474)

10.7g 21mm
1912,0709.227 Bleazby collection

477
Silver rupee with a leaf and the numeral 9 on the reverse

AD 1832/VS 1889
Authority: Ranjit Singh
Inscription: Gobindshahi couplet (as no. 474)

8.4g 20mm
1936,1017.12 Baldwin collection

478
Silver rupee with a leaf on the reverse

AD 1831/VS 1888
Authority: Governor Bhima Singh
Inscription: Gobindshahi couplet (as no. 474)
Persian letter ب 'B' for Bhima Singh on the obverse

10.7g 21mm
1912,0709.228 Bleazby collection

479
Silver rupee with a tiger, a punch dagger and a leaf on the reverse
The tiger on the reverse represents Sher Singh [sher meaning tiger or lion]

AD 1833/VS 1890
Authority: Governor Sher Singh
Inscription: Gobindshahi couplet (as no. 474)

8.3g 20mm
1936,1017.44 Baldwin collection

480
Silver rupee with a leaf on the obverse and a punch dagger on the reverse

AD 1834/VS 1891
Authority: Governor Sher Singh
Inscription: Gobindshahi couplet (as no. 474)

8.4g 20mm
1936,1017.53 Baldwin collection

481
Silver rupee with a sword and shield symbol on the obverse and a leaf on the reverse
The sword and shield symbol represents the Governor Mihan Singh

AD 1834/VS 1891
Authority: Governor Mihan Singh
Inscription: Gobindshahi couplet

Obverse: Persian

دیگ و تیغ و فتح و نصرت بیدرنگ یافت از نانک گورو گوبند سنگ

Transliteration
Deg o tegh o fath o nusrat bedrang Yaft az Nanak Guru Gobind Singh

Translation
Abundance, power and victory [and] assistance without delay are the gift of Nanak [and] Guru Gobind Singh

Reverse: Persian

ضرب کشمیر سری اکال پور که جیب

Transliteration
Zarb Kashmir Sri Akal Pur Jib

Translation
Struck in Kashmir, in the city of the timeless One

11.0g 20mm
1936,1017.46 Baldwin collection

482
Silver rupee with a sword and shield symbol and a leaf on the reverse

AD 1836/VS 1893
Authority: Governor Mihan Singh
Inscription: Gobindshahi couplet (as no. 481)

10.9g 22mm
1920,0514.75 Doyle Smithe collection

483
Silver rupee with a sword and shield symbol and a leaf on the reverse

AD 1837/VS 1894
Authority: Governor Mihan Singh
Inscription: Gobindshahi couplet (as no. 481)

10.7g 21mm
1912,0709.229 Bleazby collection

484
Silver rupee with a sword and shield symbol and a leaf on the reverse

AD 1838/VS 1895
Authority: Governor Mihan Singh
Inscription: Gobindshahi couplet (as no. 481)

10.7g 21mm
1936,1017.49 Baldwin collection

485
Silver rupee with a sword and shield symbol and a leaf on the reverse

AD 1839/VS 1896
Authority: Governor Mihan Singh
Inscription: Gobindshahi couplet (as no. 481)

10.8g 20mm
1912,0709.230 Bleazby collection

486
Silver rupee with a sword and shield symbol and a leaf on the reverse

AD 1840/VS 1897
Authority: Governor Mihan Singh
Inscription: Gobindshahi couplet (as no. 481)

11.0g 22mm
1936,1017.47 Baldwin collection

487
Silver rupee with a sword and shield symbol and a leaf on the reverse

AD 1841/VS 1898
Authority: Governor Mihan Singh
Inscription: Gobindshahi couplet (as no. 481)

10.9g 22mm
1936,1017.48 Baldwin collection

488
Silver rupee with a sword and shield symbol and a leaf on the reverse

AD 1837/VS 1894
Authority: Governor Mihan Singh
Inscription: Gobindshahi couplet (as no. 481)

11.0g 23mm
1860,1220.513 Hay collection

489
Silver rupee with a sword and shield symbol and a leaf on the reverse

AD 1836/VS 1893
Authority: Governor Mihan Singh
Inscription: Gobindshahi couplet (as no. 481)

10.9g 21mm
1929,0620.55 Imperial Institute collection

490
Silver rupee with a plant symbol on the obverse and a leaf on the reverse
Persian letter ش 'Shin' for Shaikh Gholam Muhyi Ud-din on the obverse

AD 1841/VS 1898
Authority: Governor Shaik Gholam Muhyi Ud-din
Inscription: Gobindshahi couplet (as no. 481)

10.7g 21mm
1936,1017.10 Baldwin collection

491
Silver rupee with a plant symbol on the obverse and a leaf on the reverse
Persian letter ش 'Shin' for Shaikh Gholam Muhyi Ud-din on the obverse

AD 1842/VS 1899
Authority: Governor Shaik Gholam Muhyi Ud-din
Inscription: Gobindshahi couplet (as no. 481)

10.4g 22mm
1920,0617.72 Ibbeston collection

Catalogue Nos 492–501

492

Silver rupee with a plant symbol on the obverse and a leaf on the reverse
Persian letter ش 'Shin' on the obverse

AD 1843/VS 1900
Authority: Governor Shaik Gholam Muhyi Ud-din
Inscription: Gobindshahi couplet (as no. 481)

10.3g   20mm
1912,0709.231 Bleazby collection

493

Silver rupee with a plant symbol on the obverse and a leaf on the reverse
Persian letter ش 'Shin' on the obverse

AD 1843/VS 1900
Authority: Governor Shaik Gholam Muhyi Ud-din
Inscription: Gobindshahi couplet (as no. 481)

10.9g   22mm
1936,1017.13 Baldwin collection

494

Silver rupee with a plant symbol on the obverse and a leaf on the reverse
Persian letter ش 'Shin' on the obverse

AD 1845/VS 1902
Authority: Governor Shaik Gholam Muhyi Ud-din
Inscription: Gobindshahi couplet (as no. 481)

10.8g   21mm
1853,0606.48 Strachey collection

495

Silver rupee with a flag on the obverse and a leaf on the reverse

AD 1825/VS 1882
Authority: Governor Diwan Chuni Lal
Inscription: Gobindshahi couplet (as no. 481)

11.1g   21mm
1912,0709.232 Bleazby collection

496

Silver rupee with a mint mark on the obverse and a leaf on the reverse
Persian letter ش 'Shin' on the obverse

AD 1846/VS 1903
Authority: Governor Shaik Iman Ud-din Amir
Inscription: Gobindshahi couplet (as no. 481)

10.7g   20mm
1936,1017.45 Baldwin collection

497

Silver rupee with a small plant on the obverse and a leaf on the reverse
Persian letter ش 'Shin' on the obverse

AD 1845/VS 1902
Authority: Governor Shaik Iman Ud-din Amir
Inscription: Gobindshahi couplet (as no. 481)

10.7g   21mm
1853,0606.49 Strachey collection

498

Silver rupee with a small plant on the obverse and a leaf on the reverse
Persian letter ش 'Shin' on the obverse

AD 1845/VS 1902
Authority: Governor Shaik Iman Ud-din Amir
Inscription: Gobindshahi couplet (as no. 481)

10.7g   20mm
1853,0606.47 Strachey collection

499

Silver rupee with a small plant on the obverse and a leaf on the reverse
Persian letter ش 'Shin' on the obverse

AD 1845/VS 1902
Authority: Governor Shaik Iman Ud-din Amir
Inscription: Gobindshahi couplet (as no. 481)

10.8g   20mm
1853,0606.50 Strachey collection

500

Silver rupee with a leaf on the reverse
Persian letter ش 'Shin' for Shaik Iman Ud-din Amir on the obverse

AD 1846/VS 1903
Authority: Governor Shaik Iman Ud-din Amir
Inscription: Gobindshahi couplet (as no. 481)

11.0g   19mm
1853,0606.51 Strachey collection

Copper coins

501

Copper paisa with a leaf on the reverse

AD 1836/VS 1893
Authority: Ranjit Singh

Obverse: Gurmukhi

ਸਿਖਾ ਨਾਨਕਸਾਹੀ

Transliteration
Sikka Nanakshahi

Translation
Nanakshahi coin

Reverse: Gurmukhi

ਜਰਬ ਕਸ਼ਮੀਰ ਸਾ ੧੮੯੩

Transliteration
Zarb Kashmir Sa 1893

Translation
Struck in Kashmir in 1893 (vs)

9.5g   22mm
OR 1724

502

Copper paisa with a flag on the reverse

AD 1828/VS 1885
Authority: Ranjit Singh

Obverse: Persian

یفت ضرب نانک

Transliteration
Yaft Zarb Nanak

Translation
The gift of the Lord Nanak

Reverse: Persian

سمبت کشمیر خطه ۱۸۸۰

Transliteration
1885 Sambat Kashmir Khitta

Translation
Struck in the Sambat year 1885 in the district of Kashmir

8.0g 20mm
1913,0401.13 Craig collection

503

Copper paisa with a leaf on the obverse and on the reverse

AD 1835/VS 1892
Authority: Ranjit Singh

Obverse: Persian

سکه نانک شاه

Transliteration
Sikka Nanak Shah

Translation
The Nanakshahi coin

Reverse: Persian

ضرب کشمیر خطه

Transliteration
Zarb Kashmir Khitta

Translation
Struck in the district of Kashmir

8.0g 22mm
1909,1007.6 Sutcliffe collection

504

Copper paisa with three leaves on the obverse and a leaf on the reverse

AD 1831/VS 1888
Authority: Ranjit Singh
Inscription: (as no. 503)

505

Copper paisa with three leaves on the obverse and a leaf on the reverse

AD 1831/VS 1888
Authority: Ranjit Singh

Obverse: Persian

نانک شاه گورو گوبند سنگه

Transliteration
Nanak shah Guru Gobind Singh

Translation
Nanak the King and Guru Gobind Singh

Reverse: Persian

کشمیر خطه ۱۸۸۸

Transliteration
1888 Kashmir Khitta

Translation
The district of Kashmir 1888

9.5g 19mm
1902,0608.340 Secretary of State for India collection

506

Copper paisa with a leaf on the reverse

AD 1833/VS 1890
Authority: Ranjit Singh

Obverse: Persian

سنه گورو گوبند ۱۸۹

Transliteration
Sanah Guru Gobind

Translation
The year 189 Guru Gobind

Reverse: Persian

فلوس کشمیر

Transliteration
Fulus Kashmir

Translation
Copper coin of Kashmir

16.5g 19mm
1912,0709.365 Bleazby collection

507

Copper paisa with a leaf on the reverse

AD 1833/VS 1890
Authority: Ranjit Singh
Inscription: (as no. 506)

16.9g 18mm
1912,0709.366 Bleazby collection

508

Copper paisa with a leaf on the reverse

AD 1833/VS 1890
Authority: Ranjit Singh
Inscription: (as no. 506)

16.0g 20mm
1912,0709.364 Bleazby collection

509

Copper paisa with flowers on the obverse and a leaf on the reverse

AD 1837/VS 1894
Authority: Ranjit Singh

Obverse: Persian

نانک

Transliteration
Nanak

Translation
Nanak

Reverse: Persian

ضرب کشمیر ۱۸۹۴

Catalogue Nos 510–517

Transliteration
Zarb Kashmir 1894

Translation
Struck in Kashmir in Sambat 1894

9.4g 24mm
1909,1007.1 Sutcliffe collection

510
Copper paisa with flowers on the obverse and a leaf on the reverse

AD 1837/VS 1894
Authority: Ranjit Singh
Inscription: (same as no. 509)

8.6g 22mm
1903,1009.58 Talbot collection

511
Copper paisa with flowers on the obverse and a leaf on the reverse

AD 1837/VS 1894
Authority: Ranjit Singh
Inscription: (same as no. 509)

9.4g 25mm
1902,0608.339 Secretary of State for India collection

512
Copper paisa with a leaf on the reverse

AD 1832/VS 1889
Authority: Ranjit Singh

Obverse: Persian
سکه گورو گوبند سنگه

Transliteration
Sikka Guru Gobind Singh

Translation
Coin of Guru Gobind Singh

Reverse: Persian
ضرب کشمیر فلوس

Transliteration
Zarb Kashmir fulus

Translation
Copper coin struck in Kashmir

12.2g 23mm
1902,0608.341 Secretary of State for India collection

513
Copper elongated paisa with a flower on the reverse

AD 1823/VS 1880
Authority: Ranjit Singh

Obverse: Persian
نانک شاه

Transliteration
Nanak Shah

Translation
The Nanakshahi coin

Reverse: Gurmukhi
ਜਰਬ ਕਸ਼ਮੀਰ

Transliteration
Zarb Kashmir

Translation
Struck in Kashmir

15.9g 20 x 29mm
1902,0615.22 Jamieson collection

514
Copper paisa

Date unobserved

Obverse: Gurmukhi
ਨਾਨਕ ਸਾਹ

Transliteration
Nanak Saha

Translation
May Nanak help

Reverse: Gurmukhi
ਜਰਬ ਕਸ਼ਮੀਰ

Transliteration
Zarb Kashmir

Translation
Struck in Kashmir

10.1g 20mm
1902,1203.38 Templer collection

515
Copper paisa with flowers on the obverse and a leaf on the reverse

AD 1837/VS 1894
Authority: Ranjit Singh
Inscription: (same as no. 509)

8.7g 20mm
1902,0608.338 Secretary of State for India collection

516
Copper paisa with three leaves on the reverse Persian letter ش 'Shin' represents Shaik Iman Ud-din Amir on the obverse

Date illegible
Authority: Governor Shaik Iman Ud-din Amir

Obverse: Persian
ضرب کشمیر

Transliteration
Zarb Kashmir

Translation
Struck in Kashmir

Reverse: Persian
اکال پرک

Transliteration
Akalpurkh

Translation
The immortal Lord

6.7g 21mm
1909,1007.2 Sutcliffe collection

517
Copper paisa with date on the obverse and a leaf on the reverse

AD 1840/VS 1897
Authority: Kharak Singh

Obverse: Persian
ضرب ۱۸۹۷

Transliteration
Zarb 1897 (vs)

68 | Catalogue of Sikh Coins in the British Museum

Translation
Struck in 1897

Reverse: Persian

اکال پرک

Transliteration
Akalpurkh

Translation
Immortal lord

7.2g   21mm
OR 5047

518
Copper paisa

Date unobserved
Authority: Unknown

Obverse: Gurmukhi

ਨਾਨਕ ਸਾਹ

Transliteration
Nanak Sah

Translation
May Nanak help

Reverse: Gurmukhi

ਜਰਬ ਕਸ਼ਮੀਰ

Transliteration
Zarb Kashmir

Translation
Struck in Kashmir

10.3g   22mm
1902,0608.343 Secretary of State for India collection

519
Copper paisa with a tiger, representation of Sher Singh on the reverse

Date unobserved
Authority: Sher Singh

Obverse: Persian

خطہ کشمیر

Transliteration
Khitta Kashmir

Translation
The district of Kashmir

10.4g   18mm
OR 2270

520
Copper half paisa with flowers on the obverse and flower dots on the reverse

AD 1830/VS 1887
Authority: Ranjit Singh
Inscription: (same as no. 412)

7.9g   19mm
1912,0709.357 Bleazby collection

521
Copper half paisa with a tiger, representation of Sher Singh on the reverse

AD 1841/VS 1898
Authority: Sher Singh

Obverse: Persian

١٨٩٨ گورو گوبند سنگہ

Transliteration
Guru Gobind Singh 1898

Translation
Guru Gobind Singh 1898

Reverse: Persian

خطہ کشمیر

Transliteration
Khitta Kashmir

Translation
The district of Kashmir

5.7g   22mm
1913,0401.9 Craig collection

522
Copper half paisa with a tiger, representation of Sher Singh on the reverse

AD 1841/VS 1898
Authority: Sher Singh

Obverse: Gurmukhi

ਨਾਨਕ ਸਾਹ

Transliteration
Nanak sah

Translation
May Nanak help

Reverse: Persian

خطہ کشمیر

Transliteration
Khitta Kashmir

Translation
The district of Kashmir

3.9g   17mm
1913,0401.14 Craig collection

523
Copper half paisa with a flower on the reverse

Date unobserved
Authority: unknown

Obverse: Persian

فلوس سکہ نلنک شاہ

Transliteration
Fulus Sikka Nanak Shah

Translation
Copper coin of the Lord Nanak

Reverse: Persian

ضرب کشمیر خطہ

Transliteration
Zarb Kashmir Khitta

Translation
Struck in the district of Kashmir

7.8g   23mm
1910,0202.6 Sutcliffe collection

524
Copper half paisa with a flag on the obverse and a leaf on the reverse

AD 1830/VS 1887
Authority: Ranjit Singh
Inscription: (as no. 523)

8.3g   19mm
1909,1007.5 Sutcliffe collection

Catalogue Nos 525–532

525

Copper half paisa with a leaf on the obverse and a leaf on the reverse

AD 1843/VS 1900
Authority: Sher Singh
Inscription: (as no. 523)

7.9g   24mm
1912,0709.363 Bleazby collection

526

Copper half paisa with a flower on the obverse

AD 1841/VS 1898
Authority: Governor Mihan Singh

Obverse: Persian

کشمیر سکه فلوس

Transliteration
Kashmir sikka fulus

Translation
The copper fulus coins of Kashmir

Reverse: Persian

جلوس مانوس ۱۸۹۸

Transliteration
Julus Manus 1898

Translation
The year of the human reign 1898

6.6g   23mm
1920,0617.68 Ibbeston collection

527

Copper half paisa with a flower on the obverse

Date off the flan
Authority: Unknown

Obverse: Persian
Illegible obverse inscription

Reverse: Gurmukhi

ਜਰਬ ਕਸ਼ਮੀਰ

Transliteration
Zarb Kashmir

Translation
Struck in Kashmir

6.5g   22mm
1903,1009.98 Talbot collection

528

Copper half paisa with date on obverse and a leaf on the reverse

AD 1840/VS 1897
Authority: Kharak Singh

Obverse: Persian

ضرب ۱۸۹۷

Transliteration
Zarb 1897 (VS)

Translation
Struck in 1897

Reverse: Persian

اکال پرک

Transliteration
Akal purkh

Translation
Immortal lord

6.9g   20mm
1912,0709.368 Bleazby collection

529

Copper half paisa with a leaf on the reverse
Persian letter ش 'Shin' for Shaik Iman Ud-din Amir on the obverse

AD 1842/VS 1899
Authority: Governor Shaik Iman Ud-din Amir
Illegible Persian Inscription

5.6g   19mm
1902,0608.344 Secretary of state for India collection

530

Copper half paisa with a mint mark on the obverse and a leaf on the reverse

AD 1840/VS 1897
Authority: Kharak Singh
Inscription: (as no. 528)

7.6g   19mm
1902,0608.342 Secretary of state for India collection

531

Copper half paisa with a leaf on the obverse and a flag on the reverse

AD 1831/VS 1888
Authority: Ranjit Singh

Obverse: Gurmukhi

ਜਰਬ ਕਸ਼ਮੀਰ

Transliteration
Zarb Kashmir

Translation
Struck in Kashmir

Reverse: Persian

ਸਮਤ ۱۸۸۸ ضرب کشمیر

Transliteration
Zarb Kahsmir Samvat 1888

Translation
Struck in Kashmir in samvat 1888
(The word 'samvat' is written in Gurmukhi)

7.8g   21mm
1903,1009.45 Talbot collection

532

Copper half paisa with a flower on the reverse

AD 1830/VS 1887
Authority: Ranjit Singh

Obverse: Persian

نانک شاه

Transliteration
Nanak Shah

Translation
The Nanak Shahi coin

Reverse: Gurmukhi

ਜਰਬ ਕਸ਼ਮੀਰ ੧੮੮੭

Transliteration
Zarb Kashmir 1887

Translation
Struck in Kashmir in 1887

7.0g   23mm
1903,1009.42 Talbot collection

533
Copper half paisa with a flower on the reverse

AD 1830/VS 1887
Authority: Ranjit Singh
Inscription: (as no. 532)

7.3g   19mm
1909,1007.3 Sutcliffe collection

534
Copper half paisa with a flower on the reverse

AD 1830/VS 1887
Authority: Ranjit Singh
Inscription: (as no. 532)

7.4g   19mm
1912,0709.367 Bleazby collection

535
Copper quarter-anna

AD 1839/VS 1896
Authority: Ranjit Singh

Obverse: Persian

نانک شاه

Transliteration
Nanak Shah

Translation
The Nanak Shahi coin

Reverse: Illegible Persian inscription

2.9g   16mm
1920,0617.67 Ibbeston collection

Mint Derajat

To view referenced mint marks, see Appendix 2.

Silver coins

536
Silver rupee with a mint mark on the obverse and leaf on the reverse

AD 1841/VS 1898
Authority: Sher Singh
Inscription: Gobindshahi couplet

Obverse: Persian

دیگ تیغ فتح نصرت بیدرنگ یافت از نانک گوروگوبند سنگ

Transliteration
Deg tegh fath nusrat bedrang Yaft az Nanak Guru Gobind Singh

Translation
Abundance, power and victory [and] assistance without delay are the gift of Nanak [and] Guru Gobind Singh

Reverse: Persian

ضرب دیره جات

Transliteration
Zarb Derajat

Translation
Minted in Derajat

10.7g   20mm
1912,0709.222 Bleazby collection

537
Silver rupee with a mint mark on the obverse and a leaf on the reverse

AD 1841/VS 1898
Authority: Sher Singh
Inscription: Gobindshahi couplet (as no. 536)

10.7g   20mm
1936,1017.43 Baldwin collection

538
Silver rupee with a leaf on the reverse

AD 1844/VS 1901
Authority: Sher Singh
Inscription: Gobindshahi couplet (as no. 536)

10.6g   18mm
1936,1017.38 Baldwin collection

Copper coins

539
Copper paisa with a leaf on the reverse

AD 1841/VS 1898
Authority: Sher Singh

Obverse: Gurmukhi

ਸ਼ੇਰ ੧੮੯੮ ਸਿਘ

Transliteration
Sher 1898 (vs) Singh

Translation
Sher Singh 1898 (vs)

Reverse: Persian

ضرب دیره

Transliteration
Zarb Dera

Translation
Struck in the town of Dera

8.1g   21mm
1885,0610.57 C.J. Rodgers collection

540
Copper fulus

AD 1841/VS 1898
Authority: Sher Singh

Obverse: Persian

راج

Transliteration
Raij

Catalogue Nos 541–546

Translation
Current

Reverse: Persian
ضرب دیره جات

Transliteration
Zarb Derajat

Translation
Fulus struck at Derajat

8.8g 19mm
1920,0617.73 Ibbetson collection

541

Copper half paisa with a leaf and flower on the reverse

AD 1839/VS 1896
Authority: Ranjit Singh
Inscription: Gobindshahi couplet (as no. 536)

7.6g 21mm
OR 5051

542

Copper half paisa with a leaf and flower on the reverse

AD 1839/VS 1896
Authority: Ranjit Singh
Inscription: Gobindshahi couplet (as no. 536)

7.6g 22mm
1860,1220.485 Hay collection

543

Copper half paisa with a leaf on the reverse

AD 1839/VS 1896
Authority: Ranjit Singh
Inscription: Gobindshahi couplet (as no. 536)

8.4g 19mm
1860,1220.607 Hay collection

Mint Nimak

To view referenced mint marks, see Appendix 2.

Silver coins

544

Silver rupee with a leaf on the reverse

AD 1848/VS 1905
Authority: Dulip Singh
Inscription: Nanakshahi couplet

Obverse: Persian and Gurmukhi
سکا زد بر هر دو عالم فضل سچا صاحب است فتح
تیغ گوروگوبند سنگ شاه نانک وهب است
राम जी म

Transliteration
Sikka zad bar har do alam fazl sacha sahib ast
Fateh tegh Guru Gobind Singh Shah, Nanak wahib ast
Ram Ji M

Translation
The coin struck through each of the two worlds by the grace of the true Lord. Of the victory gained by the sword of Guru Gobind Singh Shah Nanak is the provider Ram Ji

Reverse: Persian
سری نمک جیو
ضرب جلوس میمنت بخت اکال تخت سنه

Transliteration
Sri Nimak jiyo zarb Julus maimanat bakht Akal Takht sanah

Translation
Struck in the Illustrious Nimak under the prosperous rule of the fortunate rule Akal Takht

11.0g 23mm
1912,0709.301 Bleazby collection

545

Silver rupee with a flower on the obverse and a leaf on the reverse

AD 1848/VS 1905
Authority: Dulip Singh
Inscription: Nanakshahi couplet (as no. 544 without the addition of the Nagri on the obverse)

11.1g 25mm
1936,1017.39 Baldwin collection

Mint Mankera

To view referenced mint marks, see Appendix 2.

Silver coins

546

Silver rupee with a leaf on the reverse

AD 1822/VS 1879
Authority: Ranjit Singh
Inscription: Gobindshahi couplet

Obverse: Persian
دیگ تیغ و فتح نصرت بیدرنگ یافت از نانک
گوروگوبند سنگ

Transliteration
Deg tegh o fath nusrat bedrang Yaft az Nanak Guru Gobind Singh

Translation
Abundance, power and victory [and] assistance without delay are the gift of Nanak [and] Guru Gobind Singh

Reverse: Persian
سمبت جلوس مانوس میمنت

Transliteration
Sambat Julus Manus Maimanat

Translation
Struck in the Sambat year during the prosperous human reign

10.9g 21mm
1936,1017.42 Baldwin collection

Appendices

Chromolithograph pictorial label showing the ten Sikh Gurus seated on a terrace with attendants. Printed on paper, early 20th century. British Museum, 2008,3020.5

Appendix 1: Sikh, Mughal and Afghan Rulers

AD	Mughal Rulers	Sikh Rulers	Afghan Rulers
1500		Guru Nanak (1469–1539)	
1510			
1520	Babur (1526–30)		
1530	Humayun (1530–40)		
1540	Suri Sultans	Guru Angad (1539–52)	
1550	Humayun (1555–56)	Guru Amar Das (1552–74)	
1560	Akbar (1556–1605)		
1570		Guru Ram Das (1574–81)	
1580		Guru Arjan (1581–1606)	
1590			
1600	Jahanghir (1605–27)	Guru Hargobind (1606–44)	
1610			
1620			
1630	Shahjahan (1628–58)		
1640		Guru Har Rai (1644–61)	
1650			

(Cont. on following page)

Sikh, Mughal and Afghan rulers (cont.)

AD	Mughal Rulers	Sikh Rulers	Afghan Rulers
1660	Aurangzeb (1658–1707)	Guru Har Krishan (1661–64)	
		Guru Tegh Bahadur (1664–75)	
1670		Guru Gobind Singh (1675–1708)	
1680			
1690			
1700			
	Shah Alam I (1707–12)	Banda Singh Bahadur (1710–16)	
1710	Jahandar Shah (1712–13)		
	Farrukhsiyar (1713–19)		
1720	Muhammad Shah (1719–48)		
1730			
1740			Nadir Shah Afsharid (1736–47)
1750	Ahmad Shah Bahadur (1748–54)		Ahmad Shah Durrani (1747–72)
	Alamgir II (1754–59)		
1760	Shah Alam II (1759–1806)	Sikh Misals (1760–1801)	
1770			Taimur Shah (1772–93)
1780			
1790			Zaman Shah (1793–1801)
1800			Mahmud Shah (1801–03)
		Maharaja Ranjit Singh (1801–39)	Shah Shuja (1803–09)
1810	Akbar Shah II (1806–37)		Mahmud Shah second reign (1809–18)
1820			Ayub Shah (1818–23)
1830			Dost Muhammad Khan Barakzai (1826–39 / 1845–63)
1840	Bahadur Shah II (1837–57)	Kharak Singh (1839–40)	
		Sher Singh (1840–43)	
1850		Dulip Singh (1843–49)	

Appendix 2: Mint marks on Sikh Coins

Mint marks on coins minted at Amritsar

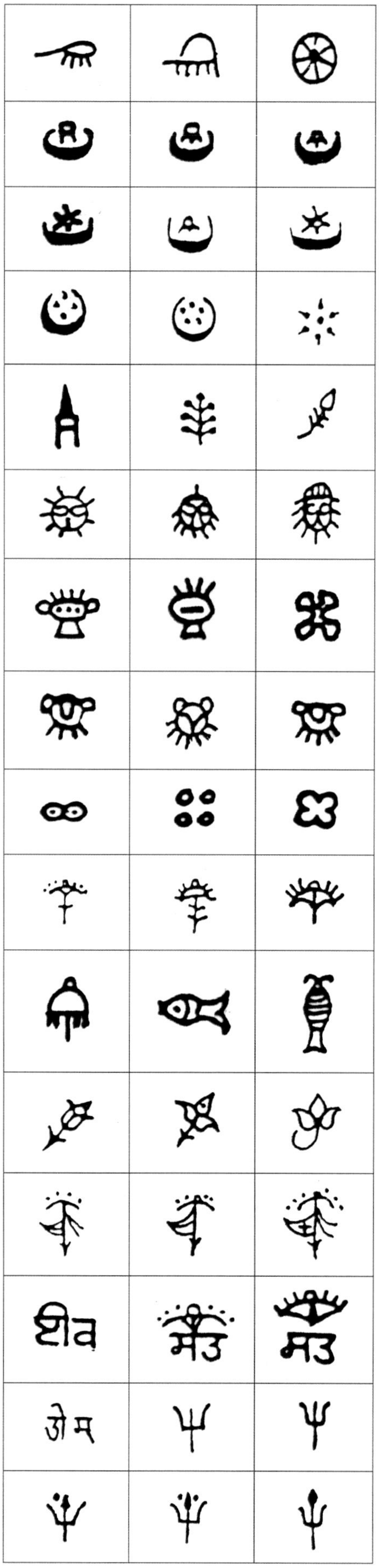

Mint marks on coin minted at Anandgarh

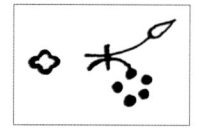

Mint marks on coins minted at Multan

FIRST OCCUPATION (1772–79)

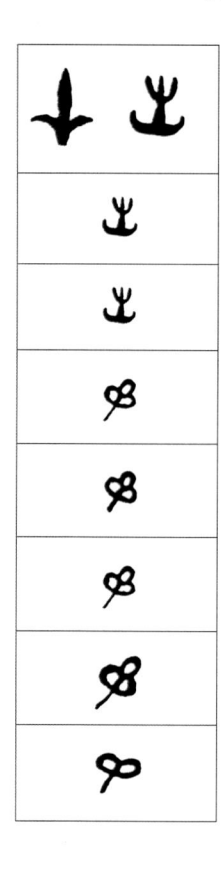

Mint marks on coins minted at Multan cont.

SECOND OCCUPATION (1818–48)

Mint marks on coins minted at Derajat

Appendix 3: Gurmukhi and Persian Numerals

	1	2	3	4	5	6	7	8	9	0
Gurmukhi	੧	੨	੩	੪	੫	੬	੭	੮	੯	੦
Persian	۱	۲	۳	۴	٥	۶	۷	۸	۹	٠

Appendix 4: Vikrama Samvat Conversion Chart

VS	AD	VS	AD	VS	AD
1800	1743	1843	1786	1885	1828
1801	1744	1844	1787	1886	1829
1802	1745	1845	1788	1887	1830
1803	1746	1846	1789	1888	1831
1804	1747	1847	1790	1889	1832
1805	1748	1848	1791	1890	1833
1806	1749	1849	1792	1891	1834
1807	1750	1808	1751	1850	1793
1892	1835	1809	1752	1851	1794
1893	1836	1810	1753	1852	1795
1894	1837	1811	1754	1853	1796
1895	1838	1812	1755	1854	1797
1896	1839	1813	1756	1855	1798
1897	1840	1814	1757	1856	1799
1898	1841	1815	1758	1857	1800
1899	1842	1816	1759	1858	1801
1900	1843	1817	1760	1859	1802
1901	1844	1818	1761	1860	1803
1902	1845	1819	1762	1861	1804
1903	1846	1820	1763	1862	1805
1904	1847	1821	1764	1863	1806
1905	1848	1822	1765	1864	1807
1906	1849	1823	1766	1865	1808
1907	1850	1824	1767	1866	1809
1908	1851	1825	1768	1867	1810
1909	1852	1826	1769	1868	1811
1910	1853	1827	1770	1869	1812
1911	1854	1828	1771	1870	1813
1912	1855	1829	1772	1871	1814
1913	1856	1830	1773	1872	1815
1914	1857	1831	1774	1873	1816
1915	1858	1832	1775	1874	1817
1916	1859	1833	1776	1875	1818
1917	1860	1834	1777	1876	1819
1918	1861	1835	1778	1877	1820
1919	1862	1836	1779	1878	1821
1920	1863	1837	1780	1879	1822
1921	1864	1838	1781	1880	1823
1922	1865	1839	1782	1881	1824
1923	1866	1840	1783	1882	1825
1924	1867	1841	1784	1883	1826
1925	1868	1842	1785	1884	1827
1926	1869				

Glossary

Adi Granth
Early compilation of the Sikh scriptures by Guru Arjun, the fifth Sikh Guru in 1604. 'Aad Granth' literally translates as half scripture. Further scriptures were added later by the successive Sikh Gurus resulting in the complete *Guru Granth Sahib*.

Akal
Term meaning immortal, timeless and non-temporal, often used as a name for God.

Akal Takht
Translates as the 'seat of the immortal' or 'seat of God'. The Akal Takht refers to the building opposite the Harimandir (Golden Temple) in Amritsar which is the seat of political authority for the Sikhs.

Amrit
Sanskrit word meaning immortality or nectar of the Gods. In Sikhism the term refers to the water by which Sikhs are baptised.

Arsi
Thumb mirror traditionally worn by dancing girls in the Punjab

Bhai
A title or form of address used for distinguished and respected Sikh men.

Baba
Persian word meaning father, this term is used as a title for respected figures in Sikhism.

Banda
Servant, slave, human being or man.

Bhatta
An Indian tax involving the devaluation of coins.

Deg, Tegh, Fateh
Slogan commonly used by Sikhs describing the essence of Sikhism. Translates literally as charity or assistance to the helpless, sword and victory.

Daswandh
Donation of a tenth of one's earnings.

Dal Khalsa
Army of the Khalsa

Diwali
Festival of light celebrated by Sikhs to commemorate 'Bandi Chor' the release of the sixth Sikh Guru, Guru Hargobind from Gwalior fort.

Fulus
Meaning 'copper coin' in Arabic, derived from Roman term Follis used for copper coins in the Byzantine Empire.

Guru
A term used to describe someone regarded as having great knowledge and wisdom, also means teacher.

Gurmukhi
Literally translates as 'from the mouth of the Guru'. The term refers to the script used to write the Punjabi language, standardised by the second Sikh Guru, Guru Angad. The entire Guru Granth Sahib is written in the Gurmukhi script.

Guru Granth Sahib
Sikh scriptures containing 1430 pages of verses complied by the Sikh Gurus, saints and holy men. The Guru Granth Sahib is the present and eternal Guru of the Sikhs. The term 'Granth' means 'scripture' and 'Sahib' meaning 'master' or 'lord'.

Gurmatta
A formal decision or resolution made in the presence of the Guru Granth Sahib.

Gobindshahi
Inscription on Sikh coins starting with the slogan 'Degh, Tegh, Fateh'.

Harimandir
Sikh holy shrine in Amritsar, also known as 'Darbar Sahib' or 'Golden Temple'. The construction of the temple was started by the fourth Sikh Guru, Guru Ram Das and was completed by his successor the fifth Sikh Guru, Guru Arjan.

Janam Sakhis
'Life stories' or accounts of the life of Guru Nanak. These accounts are believed to have been written by Guru Nanak's companion, Bhai Bala.

Kaur
Mandatory last or middle name for Sikh females meaning 'princess'. This name was given to all Sikh women at the Khalsa initiation ceremony in 1699.

Khera

Khanda
A double edged sword used to stir the ambrosial nectar at the Khalsa baptism ceremony in April 1699.

Khalsa
The collective body of all baptised Sikhs, the military order of saint soldiers established by the tenth Guru, Guru Gobind Singh in 1699.

Katar
Punch dagger

Kirpan
A sword or dagger

Langar
Free kitchen for the poor, initiated by Guru Nanak

Lakh
Unit of 100,000.

Misal
A term to describe a unit or part of a collective body. The Sikh Misals also referred to as confederacies were 12 divisions that controlled different regions of the Punjab from 1760–1801.

Mohur
Gold denomination of a Sikh coin

Moran
Name of a dancing girl in the court of Ranjit Singh, Moran meaning peacock

Nazrana
Gift or ceremonial piece

Nimak
Punjabi and Urdu word meaning Salt

Nanakshahi
Term referring to the coins that have the 'Nanakshahi' inscription, starting 'Sikka zad…'

Pandit
A Sanskrit word meaning scholar or one who is particularly skilled in the Sanskrit language and has mastered the Hindu Vedic scriptures

Paisa
Copper denomination of a Sikh coin

Pipal
A sacred fig tree also known as the *ficus religiosa*

Rahit
The code of conduct that Sikhs live by

Rupee
Silver denomination of a Sikh coin

Sadhu
A term referring to a holy man, ascetic or wondering monk

Sangat
Meaning fellowship, company or congregation

Sacha Sahib
Literal translation 'true master' a reference to God or the divine

Sarbat Khalsa
Entire body of Sikhs that met twice a year during the Sikh misal period

Sikh
Learner, student or disciple

Singh
Mandatory last name or middle name for Sikh males meaning 'lion'. This name was given to all Sikh men at the Khalsa initiation ceremony in 1699.

Sardar
A title of Persian origin used for Indian princes, noblemen and aristocrats.

Taxsali/Taksal
A term referring to the place where coins are minted

Trisul
Meaning trident of three pronged fork

Vaisakhi
Punjabi harvest festival coinciding with the formation of the Khalsa in 1699.

Vikrama Samvat
According to Indian tradition, the Vikrama Samvat calendar was established by the Indian Emperor Vikramaditya of Ujjain (102 BC–AD 15), after his victory over the Sakas in 56 BC This calendar is used by most Sikhs and Hindus in North India.

Zafarnama
The epistle of victory sent by Guru Gobind Singh, the tenth Sikh Guru to the Mughal Emperor Aurangzeb.

Bibliography

Akbar, Muhammad, 1948. *The Punjab Under the Mughals*. Lahore: Ripon Printing Press.

Anand, Mulk Raj, 1981, *Maharja Ranjit Singh as Patron of the Arts*. Bombay: Marg Publications.

Bala, Shashi, 2006. *Relevance of Guru Granth Sahib (in the modern context)*. Amritsar: Singh Brothers.

Biddulph, C.H. 1963. 'Countermarked Durrani and Sikh Coins', *Journal of the Numismatic Society of India* 25, 198–9.

Burnes, A. 1833. 'On the commerce of central Asia', *Calcutta Monthly Journal* (1833), 306–66.

Chatterji, Chhanda. 2007, 'Sikh Coinage, State Formation and the Sovereignty in Eighteenth Century: Punjab', *Journal of Numismatic Society of India*, 69, parts 1 and 2, 152–7.

Chattopadhyay, Bhaskar, 1977. *Coins and Icon – A Study in Indian Numismatic Art*. Calcutta: Punthi Pustak.

Chopra, Gulshan Lall. 1928, *The Punjab as a Sovereign State (1799–1839)*. Lahore: Uttar Chand Kapur & Sons.

Codrington, O. 1904, *A Manual of Musalman Numismatics*. London: The Royal Asiatic Society.

Cunningham, J.D. 1915, *History of the Sikhs*. Amritsar: Satvic, Printwell, [1st edn 1849; revised edn 1915; reprint 2005].

Dance, L. 1981. 'Coinage of the Sikh Empire – An Outline', in Anand, 1981, 131–4.

Daljeet, Dr. 2004. *The Sikh Heritage: a search for totality*. New Delhi: Prakash Book Depot.

Goran, S. and Wiggens, K. 1981–84, 'The gold and silver coinage of the Sikhs', *Oriental Numismatics Society*, Parts 1–4.

Griffin, Lepel H. 1892. Sir. *Rulers of India – Ranjit Singh*. Oxford: Clarendon Press.

Gupta, Hari Ram, 1944, *Studies in the Later Mughal History of the Punjab (1707–1793)*. Lahore: Minerva Book Shop.

Gupta, Hari Ram, 1978, *History of the Sikhs*. New Delhi: Munshiram Manoharlal.

Gupta, Parmeshwari Lal, 1979. *Coins*. New Delhi: National Book Trust, [reprint of 2nd edn].

Handa, Devendra. 1996. 'Copper Coins of Sher Singh', *Oriental Numismatics Studies* 1, 193–8.

Haim, S. 2008. *Persian-English Dictionary*. New Delhi: Star Publications.

Herrli, H. 2004. *The Coins of the Sikhs*. New Delhi: Munshiram Manoharlam [2nd rev. edn].

Khokhar, Masood ul-Hasan, 1987–88. 'Origin and development of Sikh coins', *Pakistan Archaeology* 23, 263–8.

Lafont, J.M. 2002. *Maharaja Ranjit Singh – Lord of the Five Rivers*. Oxford: Oxford University Press.

Lal, Mohan Esq. 1986 (reprint). *Travels in the Punjab, Afghanistan, and Turkistan, to Balkh, Bokhara and Heart: and a visit to Great Britain and Germany*. New Delhi: Nirmal Publishers and Distributers.

Lane-Pool, S. 1892, *The Coins of the Moghul Emperors of Hindustan in the British Museum*. London: Trustees of the British Museum.

Masson, C. 1974. *Narrative of Various Journeys in Balochistan, Afghanistan and the Punjab*, vol. 1. Oxford: Oxford University Press.

McLeod, W.H. 1989. *The Sikhs – History, Religion and Society*. New York: Columbia University Press.

Mitchner, M. 1977. *Oriental Coins and their Values, The World of Islam*. London: Hawkins Publications.

Nabha, Kahan Singh, 2006, *'Mahan Kosh' Encyclopaeidia of Sikh Literature*. New Delhi: National Book Shop.

Osborne, W.G. 2002, *Ranjit Singh – Lion of the Punjab*. New Delhi: Rupa and Co.

Pall, S.J.S. 2001, *The Living of a Gursikh*. Amritsar: B. Chattar Singh Jiwan Singh.

Rai, Jyoti, 1995, 'Rediscovering Sikh Mints – Peshawar, Dera, Rawalpindi', *Oriental Numismatic Society Newsletter* 146, 13.

Rai, Jyoti, 2001. 'The divine coinage of the Sikhs', *Nishaan*, 2, 18–37.

Raijasbir Singh, 1995. 'Sikh Misal Coins minted in the Ganga Doab: A Study', *Journal of the Numismatic Society of India* 58, 124–5.

Raijasbir Singh, 1995, 'A Symbolic Study of Punjab Coins under Ranjit Singh', *Journal of the Numismatic Society of India* 52, parts 1 and 2, 124–5.

Raijasbir Singh, 1991. 'Dasam Granth and the Coinage under Aurangzeb', *Journal of the Numismatic Society of India* 53, parts 1 and 2, 190–91.

Raijasbir Singh, 1990. 'Sikh Coins and Medieval Gumukhi Literature of Punjab during the Misal Period (1751–1799)', *Journal of the Numismatic Society of India*, 52, parts 1 and 2, 40–1.

Raijasbir Singh, 1994. 'Early English and Persian writings and the Sikh coinage', *Punjab History Conference Proceedings*, 26th session, March 1994, 132–3.

Raijasbir Singh, 1987. 'Sikh misl coins and seals: A study of legends', *Punjab History conference Proceedings*, 21st session, March 1987, 129–31.

Rodgers, C.J. 1881. 'On the coins of the Sikhs', *Journal of Asiatic Society of Bengal*, 50, 71–93.

Rodgers, C.J. 1893. *Catalogue of the Coins of the Mogul Emperors of India*. Calcutta: Inter-India Publications.

Rodgers, C.J. 1885. 'The Coins of Ahmad Shah Abdalli', *Journal of Asiatic Society of Bengal* 54, part 1, 67–76.

Rodgers, C.J. 1894. *Coin Collecting in Northern India*. Allahabad: Pioneer Press.

Shan, H.S. 1969–70. *Guru Nanak in his own words*. Amritsar: Chief Khalsa Diwan.

Singh, Bhagat. 1993, *A History of the Sikh Misals*. Patiala: Punjabi University.

Singh, Ganda. 1981, *'Lion Victor of Battles', Maharaja Ranjit Singh – A Life Sketch,* in Anand 1981, 27–42.

Singh, Gopal. 1960, *Sri Guru Granth Sahib* (English), Volume 1 (revised modern idiom). New Delhi: Allied Publishers.

Singh, Jodh. 1998, *Varan Bhai Gurdas – Text, Transliteration and Translation, vol. 2*. New Delhi: Vision & Venture.

Singh, Kirpal. 2004, *Janamsakhi tradition, an analytical study*. Amritsar: Singh Brothers.

Singh, Patwant and Rai, Jyoti. M. 2008, *Empire of the Sikhs, the Life and Times of Maharaja Ranjit Singh*. London: Peter Owen Publishers.

Singh, Pashaura. 2000, *The Guru Granth Sahib: Canon, Meaning and Authority*. Oxford: Oxford University Press.

Singh, Gurprit. 2002–03, 'Coins of the Sikhs: Some interesting facts', *Journal of Numismatic Society of India* 64–65, 100–3.

Singh, Surinder. 2001 'The Earliest Sikh Coin: Imprint of a Saga', *Sikh Review* 49(7), 33–9.

Singh, Surinder. 2004, *Sikh Coinage – Symbol of Sikh Sovereignty*. New Delhi: Manohar.

Somaiya, R.T. 1994, 'Sikh Coins', *Indian Coins Society Newsletter* 25, March, 1–2.

Stronge, S. 2002, *The Arts of the Sikh Kingdoms*. London: V&A Publications.

Valentine, W.H. 1920, *The Copper Coins of India Part II, The Punjab and Contiguous Native States*. London: Spink and Son, Ltd.

Whitteridge, G. 1986, *Charles Masson of Afghanistan*. Aris & Phillips Ltd, Warminster.

On line resources
www.sikhcoins.in
www.sikhcoins.com

Index

A
Akal Takht 3, 10, 17, 20, 22, 24, 64, 72, 79
Amritsar 1, 3, 4, 5, 6, 9, 10, 11, 14, 16, 17, 18, 19, 20, 21
Anandpur 3, 4, 10
Anglo-Sikh War 8

B
Bhai Bala 2, 79
Babur 2, 10, 74
Bhai Mardana 2
Bhai Lehna 2
Bleazby, George B. 1

C
canopies 20, 21
Cis-Sutlej states 1, 6, 8
commemorative coins 1
copper coins 1, 10, 11, 14, 16, 18, 21

D
Dogra Rajas 1
Daulat Khan Lodhi 2
Durrani, Ahmed Shah 4, 6, 10, 11, 12, 17, 75
Durrani 4, 9, 10, 11, 12, 14, 17, 18, 20, 75

E
East India Company 1, 6, 9

F
flags 19, 20

G
Gobindshahi 10, 16, 18, 19
Government of India Act 1
Gurmukhi 2, 3, 16, 18, 78, 79
Guru Nanak 2, 3, 16, 17, 18
Guru Gobind Singh 4, 5, 10, 16, 17, 18, 74, 79, 80
Guru Granth Sahib 2, 4, 5, 8, 18, 20, 79

H
Herrli, Hans 1, 10, 16, 17, 19, 20

I
Indian Civil Service 1
India Office 1, 62
Iraq 2

J
Janam Sakhi 2, 79

K
Kashmir 1, 4, 6, 9, 11, 12, 20, 21
Khatri 2, 8
Khalsa 4, 5, 8, 16, 19, 79, 80

L
Lahore 1, 2, 3, 4, 5, 6, 9, 10, 11, 12, 13, 14, 19
leaf 19, 20, 21

M
Maharaja Ranjit Singh 1, 6, 10, 11, 13, 14, 16, 18, 20, 21, 75
Masson, Charles 9, 10, 11
medals 1
Mehta Kalu 2
Misal 1, 4, 5, 6, 9, 10, 11, 12, 14, 16, 19, 20, 80
Modikhana 2, 8
Mughal Emperor 2, 3, 4, 10, 12, 20, 80
Multan 1, 4, 9, 11, 12, 76, 77
Monotheistic 2

N
National Art Collections Fund 1
Nanaki 2
Nanakshahi 16, 17, 18, 80

P
peacock tail 20
Peshawar 1, 6, 9, 10, 12, 13, 17, 21
Pakistan 2

R
Rai Bhullar Bhatti 1
Rodgers, C.J. 1, 16, 20

S
Sadhus 2
silver rupees 1, 5, 12, 14, 19, 80
Singh, Surinder 1, 16, 19
Sri Lanka 2, 19

T
tokens 1
tridents 20, 80

V
Van Den Bergh, Henry 1
Vikrama Samvat 12, 19

W
Whitehead, Richard B. 1